"Here is Julie Davis at her best: reading stories and telling stories. She knows that narrative is the lifeblood of a family. She shows us where we fit in God's grand scheme. The words of the prophets were music and poetry when they were first delivered. They hit the heart with a wallop — in this retelling they still do. Highly recommended."

Mike Aquilina, executive vice-president,
St. Paul Center for Biblical Theology

"With *Thus Sayeth the Lord: A Fresh Take on the Prophets*, gifted author Julie Davis offers an innovative perspective on a time-honored but often misunderstood tradition in our Church. Accessibly executed with terrific storytelling and useable takeaways, this book helps us learn ever-current lessons from ancient prophets, while keeping our hearts open to new encounters with modern prophetic opportunities."

Lisa M. Hendey, Author of *I Am God's Storyteller*

"Julie Davis's latest book is an energetic, wise, and utterly delightful look at the biblical prophets, a guide that explores why these holy men and women are relevant today and why they are so important in the development of our own spiritual lives. *Thus Sayeth the Lord* not only informs, it entertains and inspires."

Gary Jansen, author of *Life Everlasting* and *MicroShifts: Transforming Your Life One Step at a Time*

"If you've run screaming from the Old Testament prophets, but you have a niggling idea that there has to be something there, this book is for you. If you find yourself wondering why those OT guys are such a hot deal, this book is for you. If you like diving into scripture so deeply that you float inside and laugh outside, this book is for you. Julie Davis has successfully and artfully woven together what we know, put it in context, and jumped in with both laughs. Enjoy! "

Sarah Reinhard, author and blogger, SnoringScholar.com

I0809134

"I hear all the time how the prophets of the Old Testament are a vast treasury waiting to be unlocked, but I've never been able to find the key. Thankfully, Julie Davis has come to the rescue with her book *Thus Sayeth The Lord*. Finally, I have a way to approach and appreciate the prophets that is clear, accessible, and captivating!"

Tommy Tighe, author of *The Catholic Hipster Handbook* and *Catholic Hipster: The Next Level*

To my Catholic Women's Book Club, where I started thinking about the prophets in the first place.

Table of Contents

Introduction

Comforting the Afflicted and Afflicting the Comfortable

And [Jesus] said, "Truly, I say to you, no prophet is acceptable in his own country."

Luke 4:24

No one likes a prophet, as Jesus pointed out. Especially if that prophet is a hometown boy who's laying a few hard truths on his neighbors. Jesus was so unacceptable that the townspeople tried to throw him off a big cliff right after he said this.

"People mad enough to throw you off a cliff" has been the prophet's fate since the beginning. It's understandable. Nowadays, we think of a prophet as someone who predicts the future; but that's not what the Hebrews expected from their prophets. The Hebrew word for prophet, *nāví*, means "mouth." So a prophet is God's "mouth," passing divine messages to the people. Prophets bring God's message of love to the downtrodden. They also bring God's correcting judgment to those who aren't on a good moral path. Throughout the Bible, prophets publicly confront political leaders, religious hypocrites, the wealthy preying on the poor, and even the entire nation of Israel for moral failings and worshiping false gods.

We all love a harsh scolding, right? Especially in public with everyone looking on. You can imagine how well this goes over with the rich and powerful. That's why the prophets usually are on the receiving end of equally powerful displeasure. It's not easy, but these prophets stand like walls of stone, doing whatever it takes to get God's message across. They do miracles. They give startling revelations about people's secrets. They tell the future. They show amazing faith and grace under fire. Their whole lives are devoted to delivering God's message of love, mercy, and warning.

As you read the Scriptures, you've got to take the prophets seriously, because there are a bunch with their very own books. Others are cunningly tucked into the middle of fascinating stories where they take center stage: Moses tells off the pharaoh, Deborah leads the Israelites into battle, Daniel solves not one but two locked-room mysteries, and Samuel is the only ghost we meet in the Bible. They're hard to pin down. When God gives them an assignment, some lean in, some lean away, and at least one runs as far and fast as he can in the other direction. In other words, it takes all sorts to make a prophet.

That's super for those ancient people. But what does it have to do with you and me, today? Say "prophet," and what comes to mind is likely an old, ragged-looking guy on a corner shouting about the end of the world. He's definitely got a big sign. He's probably waving it around.

We've lost touch with what it meant to encounter a prophet, or to be one. Let's take a fresh look at the familiar prophets in our Bible. Every single one has a message for us in our lives today, because that's how God rolls. He's a multitasker, and the Bible is one of his main tools in speaking to us. Those very same prophets aren't just for everyone who came before. They're for us, too. These ancient, Hebrew prophets can help bring us closer to God's love and his purpose in our lives — right here, right now.

This might not sound exciting, I know. The prophets go on and on about politics we don't understand. They make promises and threats using images we can't visualize. And they rack up quite a page count doing it. But once we know what those voices are saying across the ages, once we hear that incredible ever-new message from God, we might find our lives changed. Lean in. Let's hear what he has to say.

A Few Useful Things

A Few Handy Terms

There's nothing I skip past faster than a page of terms and definitions in a book. But there's nothing I flip back to faster when I realize I don't know everything.

And since you'd hate to read the same explanations over and over in every section, almost as much as I'd hate to write them, I'll just store these in this handy spot against future need. Enjoy!

Prophet

"Prophet" in Hebrew means "mouth." God speaks through these men and women. They're found scattered throughout the historical books of the Bible, usually sent to get the Chosen People back on track whenever they went off the rails. Most prophets were too busy to write things down, but a few took the time to set their thoughts down on paper or passed the job on to secretaries. Their books are named after them and are called either "major" or "minor."

Major prophet

"Major" means the book is long. It isn't about how important a prophet is, though each had a lot to say, and you'll probably recognize most of the names. We'll hit almost all of them: Isaiah, Jeremiah, Ezekiel, and Daniel. (The one we're not covering: Jeremiah's secretary Baruch.)

Minor prophet
"Minor" means the book is short; but while definitely more succinct, these guys are just as relevant as the more long-winded prophets. We'll meet four of the twelve minor prophets: Hosea, Amos, Habakkuk, and Jonah.

Prophet guild
Prophets were often organized into guilds, which trained and maintained prophetic traditions. Some of the Old Testament prophets (for example, the prophet Amos, whom we'll talk about later) went out of their way to be sure people knew they were independent of these groups.

Who Wrote What

Some books of the Bible, such as Psalms, were put together by editors. Some books were traditionally assumed to have been written by the people they're named after, especially the prophetic books. Newfangled scholarship has changed a lot of the traditional ideas about authorship, which has led to a lot of arguments and arm-waving. We're gonna keep it simple. I'm more interested in what the books say than who specifically wrote them down. I'm generally going with the traditional authorship when it comes up. (Which won't be often, don't worry.)

Super-fast Biblical History

You don't need tons of history to get to know the prophets; but a little is helpful, as most of them are talking about religion and politics.

The Jewish tribes settled as a nation in Israel around 1500 B.C. They were a loose conglomeration of tribes guided by the occasional leader, or "judge," who stepped up whenever a crisis arose. They eventually established a monarchy, and hit their glory days in 1000 B.C. under King David and his son Solomon. When Solomon died, the country split into two kingdoms: Israel in the north (made up of ten tribes) and Judah in the south (the tribes of Judah and Benjamin). Three hundred years later, Israel was destroyed by Assyria. About a hundred years later, Judah was destroyed by the Babylonians. Some of the population was enslaved and taken to Babylon in what was called, appropriately enough, the Babylonian Captivity or Exile. Fifty years later, they were allowed to return to the ruins that war had made of their temple and country.

Along with commenting on current events, the prophets began hinting at the coming of the Messiah, a national hero who would finally fix things once and for all by creating heaven on earth. Now *that's* what I'm talking about!

Apocalyptic Literature

A specifically Jewish and Christian genre describing God's plan for the world up through the end times. It usually has weird, imaginative visions combining fantasy and reality. It's meant to give people hope during times of trial and great troubles. The prophets invented this, and we've got some mind-bending reading ahead of us.

Hebrew Poetry

Some prophets loved writing their predictions as poems. Hebrew poetry doesn't rhyme; instead, it uses parallels to reinforce thoughts and make an impact with creative repetition. You thought free verse was something new? Nope, it's from Mesopotamian times, and probably even earlier. It was the style of the times, and the prophets did it better than anyone.

There are different sorts of parallels, but I promise they are easy to pick up without taking a whole class on Hebrew poetry.

> My mouth shall speak wisdom;
> the meditation of my heart shall be understanding.
> (Ps 49:3)

The second line above parallels the point of the first, but by repeating the thought in different words that enrich and beautify.

A second method is to parallel by using contrasting or negative imagery to make the first point even stronger:

> A wise man's heart inclines him toward the right,
>   but a fool's heart toward the left. (Eccl 10:2)

Last but not least is a method where the second part completes the thought from the first line:

> As a hart longs
>   for flowing streams,
> so longs my soul
>   for thee, O God. (Ps 42:1)

I don't love poetry, and I don't love free verse, but I began to enjoy Hebrew poetry once I discovered those parallels.

Now, let's get to the good stuff.

Chapter 1

Moses

Eighty-Year-Old Freedom Fighter

The LORD spoke with you face to face at the mountain, out of the midst of the fire, while I stood between the LORD and you at that time, to declare to you the word of the LORD; for you were afraid because of the fire, and you did not go up into the mountain.

Deuteronomy 5:4–5

What to Read

- Exodus 1–20
- Numbers 11–14, 20
- Deuteronomy 31, 34
- Acts 7:17–44 (Right before he is martyred, Saint Stephen gives a quick overview of Moses' life.)

Go-between for the people and the Lord. I never thought of Moses like that, but it's basically his main job description. After all, a prophet is the "mouth of God."

Moses is so busy changing the world that it's easy to get distracted by the fast-paced action and show-stopper miracles in his story. This guy single-handedly wrests a zillion slaves free and leads them on a forty-year trek. He teaches them their faith. Oh yeah, and makes them into a cohesive nation. While on the run. In the desert. No wonder I missed the whole prophet thing before.

Good thing God picked a superhero to handle this situation, right? Except, as usual, God isn't doing what anyone expects. Superheroes usually have incredible strength, fighting skills, and few, if any, weaknesses.

Moses isn't "super." He's all too human — his compassion, trust, and obedience are countered by insecurity, impatience, and despair. God's got the plan and the power, but he loves working through flawed, inadequate people. Moses fills that bill precisely.

Quick Take on Moses

We know this epic from the movies. The Hebrews have been slaves in Egypt for four hundred years, and they're doing pretty well. Really, they're prospering. Pharaoh's worried — so many slaves are a recipe for revolution. He orders newborn Hebrew boys drowned. (Ugh.) One clever mother puts her little guy into a basket on the river. Pharaoh's daughter rescues him and names him Moses. He's in a sweet spot to help his people get free peacefully, once he grows up and has power in the royal family.

Fast forward to forty-year-old Moses murdering an Egyptian for beating a Hebrew. So much for changing the system from the inside. He runs from the law to Midian, where he blends with local culture, becoming a shepherd and family man.

Fast forward another forty years. On the mountain with his flock, Moses is checking out this bush that's burning. He's used to brush fires, but this one's weird. The fire is not actually burning the bush. And then it gets biblical. "God called to him out of the bush, 'Moses, Moses!' And he said, 'Here am I.'" The way Moses says it, "Here I am" means "Ready and willing!" God and Moses have a Q&A with more up-close-and-personal details from God than any other episode I can think of in the Old Testament.

Moses gets a new job assignment: free the Hebrew people. He's not crazy about the idea. He's no spring chicken, after all. But you try winning an argument with the Creator of the Universe when his mind is made up. It's back to Egypt, with brother Aaron as backup.

Pharaoh's stubborn. Moses is stubborner. Moses says, "Let my people go." Pharaoh says, "I'm not listening." And God says, "Really? Try this," and sends a plague to get Pharaoh's attention. Back and forth they go, ten times, and the plagues keep getting more intense — frogs, locusts, boils, fiery hail, and so much other fun stuff. After the death of every firstborn in Egypt (except the Hebrews, of course), Pharaoh gives up.

A huge number of Hebrews take off for an epic road trip. (Numbers vary from six thousand to six million. No matter how you slice it, that's a lot of people to wrangle!)

Step one: Outrun Pharaoh's chariots, because he's changed his mind and wants his slaves back. They're trapped next to the Red Sea. God and Moses hold off the enemy and part the waters so the Hebrews can get across. Then the chariots start through, and right when they're in the middle, the waters come crashing down, drowning all the Egyptians. I'll never understand Pharaoh's strategy on that one. He hasn't figured out yet which side God is on?

Moses leads the Hebrews to the holy mountain, and God gives Moses the Ten Commandments for right living and a good life. Meanwhile, the people worry because Moses has been gone a while. They make a golden calf to worship, like you do when you've got too much time on your hands. Punishment follows. So much punishment.

Next, it's off to the promised land. The people turn down the chance to waltz right in and take over. Can you believe this? Option two is forty years of wandering in the wilderness, where they spend all their time complaining about accommodations and amenities. Finally, at age 120, Moses gets to Mount Nebo, where he can look over at the land that will become Israel. After a heartfelt farewell telling the people to love the Lord — a speech so good that Jesus quoted from it three times when rejecting the devil's temptations in the wilderness — Moses dies.

Living with Moses

God Doesn't Mind Hanging Out in a Bush. He Knows Who He Is.

The first story we hear of adult Moses is brief and shocking. Watching his own people at hard labor, he sees an Egyptian beating one of them. No one's watching, so he kills the Egyptian and hides him in sand. (He's sneakier than I expected.) The next day, he tries to break up a fight between two Hebrews only to get the third degree: "Who are you to talk, Mr. Murderer?" Hold on. If the slaves know about the murder, then what has Pharaoh heard? Oh yeah, word travels fast. Moses hightails it out of the country. It's nothing but sheep for forty years. So much for his promising career.

Exodus isn't just the story of the Hebrews becoming a nation. It's also Moses' personal growth story. He doesn't have great people skills on the construction site, so there must be something about that second life as a shepherd that prepares him for God showing up in a bush. OK, it has an unusual burning style, but it's a bush. That's not really what you expect from a god. It's a clue for Moses and for us. The one true God's got no need to get showy. He knows who he is, and pretty soon everyone else will, too.

Exodus isn't just the story of the Hebrews becoming a nation.

To become more holy is to become more authentically who we are. Holiness means stripping away the things that keep us from knowing God and learning his will. We're imperfect, and that's hard. But God does his greatest work through frail people. He helps us become the people we are meant to be.

That's the process we watch Moses undergo as he stands up to do the impossible under God's orders time after time. While he frees the Hebrews, shepherds them around the wilderness, and picks up commandments on the holy mountain, God is working with him to mold him into who he should be: "Now the man Moses was very humble, more than anyone else on earth."

Humility means seeing the truth about myself. What are my

strengths? My weaknesses? Where do these put me in relationship with others? And with God? As Saint Teresa of Calcutta pointed out, "If you are humble, nothing will touch you, neither praise nor disgrace, because you know what you are. If you are blamed, you will not be discouraged. If they call you a saint, you will not put yourself on a pedestal."

How do I get there?

Regular reflection on each day's events comes in handy. When I do this prayerfully, considering both good and bad, then I can see God's hand in my day. I can learn to be honest with myself about the good, the bad, and the ugly. It brings me closer to him and to knowing myself better.

You Can Take the Boy Out of Egypt …

Fifteen months after leaving Egypt, the Hebrews make it to the promised land. Moses sends in twelve spies to check out the situation. Good news — it's flowing with milk and honey (and delicious fruit). Bad news — it's got fortified cities, powerful people, and giants. But two of the spies have a different story. They say that the people can take these cities. God's on their side, so there's no need to worry. No one listens. One more time everyone moans, "Would it not be better for us to go back to Egypt?" Seriously? No wonder God says that this generation will have to live in the wilderness until they die off and their children can settle in the promised land.

It seems as if all anyone does is grumble to Moses about the good old days. Yes, those good old slavery days, when they had good food and no marching every day. The fact that they were also … you know … *slaves*, is something they seem to have forgotten.

In fact, this is the problem. The Hebrew people have a slave mentality. What does that mean? They have to survive the present, so they live for the moment. They cling to security and predictability because their world is a harsh, unpredictable place. Decisions are made for them, so they are unused to thinking for themselves. In an uncertain world, traveling through the wilderness, they lack confidence.

Forty years of wandering in the wilderness isn't a punishment. It's a solution. First, toughen them up with some desert living. Second, train them in a new way of thinking. This is going to take another generation, because the current adults' old habits are too deeply ingrained.

I love that God gets them to their promised land so fast. I bet that if they had marched in, the inhabitants' surprise would have made conquest easy. I also love that God respects their limitations so much that he doesn't force anything. You're not ready? OK, we'll start boot camp. Most of you won't make it out alive, but the ones who do are going to be mighty warriors. Oh, and the inhabitants might be harder to beat then, but you can't have everything.

Clearly, God will work within whatever limitations we set up. When we demand safety, predictability, and a sure thing, then we severely limit what we will accept from him. We make our own lives much harder than they need to be.

What do I place my trust in? Where does my faith lie? Do I turn God away because of my fear, instead of believing he has my best interests at heart?

Miracles Won't Change Minds

Can you believe the Hebrews made that golden calf just because Moses was a little overdue? C'mon, people. The Red Sea parted for you and drowned the enemy for you. Ten different plagues afflicted Egypt to get you out of there. Breakfast and dinner have been dropping from the sky to your doorstep like clockwork.

I know I'm not the only one who's wondered why the people went off the rails so fast even with all that glitzy evidence of God all around them. Maybe the people's slave mentality is why there's so little trust or faith. But we get evidence of people from all different backgrounds throughout the Bible not being swayed by miracles.

Even Moses isn't immune. A burning bush *talks* to him, for goodness' sake, but he begins raising objections. He's not important enough. He can't speak well enough. He doesn't know God's name. He needs to renew his library card. (OK, not really, but he's pulling out all the excuses.) Moses sweats the small stuff because his trust and faith aren't there, miracle or no miracle.

As Moses steps out in faith, he begins to experience God's faithfulness. That emboldens him to trust more quickly, to do more. The back-and-forth of a personal relationship with God draws Moses closer and powers all those miracles. So if miracles don't instantly convert people, then what's the point of them?

Miracles reveal something of God's nature, such as his generosity in feeding the Hebrews bread and meat for forty years in the desert. Miracles can show someone is authentically God's representative, such as when Moses was dealing with Pharaoh. Ultimately, they should draw us closer to God. But we have to be willing to receive the message, to believe, to trust.

The age of miracles is not past. My husband and I experienced an actual nature-doesn't-work-this-way miracle. It was a lavish sign of God's love in a time of desperation. I told only a few people about it who I thought might benefit from the bigger message of God working in the world. They were quick to write it off to coincidence or to take part of the credit for themselves. I'm no Moses, but I never felt more sympathy for him than after that experience. Moses is my reminder that it's not about the glitz. It's about the one-on-one with God.

Chapter II

Miriam

The Dancing Prophetess

O my people, what have I done to you?
In what have I wearied you? Answer me!
For I brought you up from the land of Egypt,
and redeemed you from the house of bondage;
and I sent before you Moses,
Aaron, and Miriam.

Micah 6:3–4

What to Read

- Exodus 2:1–10; 15:20–21
- Numbers 12; 20:1

About fifteen hundred years after Exodus, a prophet named Micah wrote this passage rebuking the Israelites. Miriam must have been top of mind for the Jewish people or they'd never have figured out who God was talking about. She's still a hot topic today. Look around the internet, and there are a fair number of Jewish women discussing Miriam. So why don't the rest of us know more about her?

Maybe we're distracted by all of little brother Moses' flashy miracles. Miriam is mentioned more than you'd think, always as the sister of Aaron and Moses — not as daughter or wife or mother. She's influential, an equal part of the prophetic team with the guys. Miriam's a prophetess, a leader, revered by the community, and a lady with a strong personality. She's also a bit of a troublemaker, but nobody's perfect.

Quick Take on Miriam

We're back to Exodus all over again, but focusing on Miriam brings a whole different perspective. Pharaoh orders all newborn Hebrew boys killed. A mother puts her baby son in a floating basket in the reeds. Big sis Miriam keeps an eye on baby brother from afar. Pharaoh's daughter picks him up — some babies have all the luck — and Miriam says she just happens to know a lady who'd be perfect for nursing the baby. Pharaoh's daughter jumps at the deal. Miriam goes running for Moses' own mom. I like what I'm seeing. This girl is brave, resourceful, and clever.

Fast forward, way forward, about eighty years. Right after the Hebrews' escape through the Red Sea, Moses leads a song of victory. Miriam, now called "the prophetess," jumps forward for the refrain with a song, dance, and tambourine. All the ladies follow her lead. It's a back-and-forth song and dance number weaving together thanks, praise, and joy. That's how you worship in the moment.

On the road, Miriam and Aaron pull a power play, claiming to be prophets equal to Moses. The Lord calls a family meeting, chews them out, and gives Miriam leprosy. Guess who's not gonna trash-talk Moses anymore?

Finally, toward the end of wandering in the desert for forty years, we hear of Miriam's death place and burial. Not many get that mention, but Miriam was just that important.

Living with Miriam

The Family That Prophesies Together …

How great must Miriam, Moses, and Aaron's parents have been? All three of their kids were prophets at the time when Israel itself was forged as a nation. Holiness must have been woven into this family's daily life. Even Moses was going to get those timeless Jewish values taught to him as long as his big sister and mother could keep a toehold in the palace.

This family couldn't have known God would choose them to help change the world. They endured attempted genocide and slavery. As the children grew, they watched as their baby brother was raised in wealth and then exiled for murder, and saw him go head-to-head in a seemingly impossible battle with one of the biggest powers in the world. But that's God for you. He's full of surprises.

As we look at our own families, we're not that different from Moses, Miriam, and Aaron. We blow wonderful opportunities, make terrible mistakes, and attempt crazy schemes. We have to cut each other slack when we don't agree and when someone seems to be going down the wrong road. I cannot imagine what Miriam said to nosy neighbors who rubbed Moses' murder charges in her face for forty years!

Sometimes we've just gotta hunker down and take God's timing, just as Miriam must have. During that forty years after Moses ran from murder charges, she must have lost all hope of ever seeing Moses alive again. Until he sprang up with a staff that turned into a snake, and with "deliverer" written all over his face. Can you imagine the unbelievable joy of that moment, of realizing that Moses is alive? That is a reward that only our families can give us.

She's a problem solver and natural leader.

There probably aren't burning bushes or escapes from Pharaoh in our futures, but how we give and receive love in our family ripples out to the world beyond our homes. That's when God surprises us. And maybe the world.

Leading Lady

Micah points to Miriam as an equal with her brothers in leadership. Thinking of that young girl watching out for her baby brother, I believe it. She's a problem solver and natural leader. In a slave community, Miriam has lots of chances to live up to her potential by serving others. The fruit of that life is seen when ninety-something-year-old Miriam joyfully leads the women in exuberant thanksgiving to God.

Not everyone is born a natural leader. I've read a lot of advice about leadership that basically boils down to the definition Jesus gave his disciples: "Let the greatest among you be as the youngest, and the leader as the servant."

Simple, maybe. Easy, no way.

Every time I've led a group, I've felt the real truth of Jesus' point. A real leader pours herself out to inspire, encourage, and help others to reach their potential in every circumstance. Making brownies with a child. Coaching volleyball. Coordinating a seventieth birthday party. Helping put on a retreat. Praising the Lord after escaping sure death at Pharaoh's hands. A real leader serves.

When you're thinking about others instead of yourself in achieving your goals, then you're living up to the model of Miriam — a real-life prophet.

The Doom of the Wagging Tongue

Just when Moses is getting this wilderness leadership thing figured out, Miriam and Aaron start a whisper campaign. First they criticize Moses' new wife; but then, the real issue comes out. "Has the Lord indeed spoken only through Moses? Has he not spoken through us also?"

That's when it hits the fan. Suddenly there's a giant column of cloud at the door, asking them to step outside for a chat. (I'm not making this up.) "You think you're Moses? Think again," God says. And when he leaves, Miriam has leprosy.

That's just like God, always punishing the woman and not touching the guy, right? Well, no. Miriam's name is always listed ahead of Aaron's in this story, which is Hebrew literary code for "she was driving the bus." This rebellion was her idea. Aaron begs Moses to ask for mercy for Miriam. When you're the humblest man on earth, which Scripture tells us Moses was, then of course you do! Her leprosy is healed, but God still confines her to a time-out for seven days.

God's punishment works on a lot of levels. It gets Miriam away from the community, so they've got a chance to get back to normal. It puts Miriam where she can think things through and get herself right with God. As a prophetess, she's got a straight line to the big man that way. The leprosy, before it's healed, is the perfect symbol of gossip — a spiritual disease that's contagious and deadly.

No matter what she's done, the people wait for her isolation to finish before they move on. I like to think it's not just because they respect her leadership, but also because they love her, warts and all.

The worst thing about gossip is that it can be a lot of fun as long as you're not the target. It's a hard habit to break because there's an almost addictive thrill of self-importance. And isn't that what Miriam and Aaron's problem is? They are making a bid for importance.

How do we fight this? It begins with self-awareness, and then turns into a fight for self-mastery. The key is humility, just like Moses has and which God might be helping Miriam attain. When the punishment is done, is Miriam humble? If so, then her mistake and punishment are actually blessings.

It's hard to think of punishment or correction as being a learning experience. For me, embarrassment and humiliation are usually just what I need to get me back in line. Oh, how I wish that weren't so. The way we accept and learn from these moments is the key to becoming more like Moses and less like pre-leprosy Miriam.

Bonus: There's not much about the last prophet in the family, Aaron, that doesn't have him just stretching out his arm or standing alongside Moses, who gets most of the dialogue. To read more about him, check out Exodus 4:10–17; 7:1–20; 16; 17:8–12. There's also a lot about Aaron's specific priestly duties. (Guess who they think wrote those parts?) We'll skip those.

Chapter III

Deborah

Kicking Ass and Taking Names

Now Deborah, a prophetess, the wife of Lappidoth, was judging Israel at that time.

Judges 4:4

What to Read

- Judges 4–5

Deborah's story is two short chapters that turn popular ideas about ancient Jews and gender roles upside down.

You know how you have bad habits, vow to reform, and then fall back into the same things over and over? Once Joshua (the leader after Moses) dies, that's the Israelites's main problem. With no single leader to keep them on the straight and narrow, the tribes fall into a recognizable cycle. They idolize pagan gods, and God lets them reap what they sow. Nearby nations invade, and God doesn't stop them. Eventually, the Israelites get the point and repent, wailing for help. God raises a hero (a.k.a. judge) to restore his people.

Although every sin-oppression-repentance spiral is depressingly the same, the heroes God raises each time are startlingly different. Trust God to handle each problem with creative flair. And he's willing to keep on doing it as long as they need. The

Book of Judges is one long, action-packed look at God and his heroes.

Deborah is one of the lesser known judges and prophets, but her short story is one of the most unusual. Among other things, the only other person in the entire Bible to be both a judge and a prophet is Samuel, so she's a rarely gifted individual.

Quick Take on Deborah

With Deborah, God is at his most surprising because, first of all, he gives the Jews an unconventional female leader. Not a man. Not someone like Miriam, who's always mentioned alongside her brothers. Deborah's a married woman, but her husband is just mentioned in passing. Her personal life isn't the point here. She sits under her palm tree in the mountains, judging Israel and laying down some of the most immediately provable prophecies in the entire Bible.

For twenty years, Israel has been in the power of the Canaanites. Their general, Sisera, is oppressing the heck out of everyone with his nine hundred iron chariots, the newest thing in military tech.

Deborah summons Israel's top general, Barak, giving him God's command to take ten thousand men and march to the Kishon River, where Sisera will be delivered into his power. Barak says, "OK, but only if you come, too." Without missing a beat, Deb replies, "No prob. But now a woman is going to kill their general. Coulda been your gig, but … there you go!"

With that intro, we all think it's going to be Deborah dealing the final blow, but surprise! It's a new player, Jael, with her handy tent peg and hammer!

It goes down like this: God sends rain, which floods right down the Kishon River and washes away those awesome chariots. All the Canaanites are slaughtered on the field of battle, except Sisera, who runs away on foot. Smart or coward? You decide.

He winds up at a tent where his ally's wife, Jael, is home alone. She offers him a jug of milk, and when he's off guard, she takes a tent peg and drives it through Sisera's temple with a big mallet. One translation says the peg went through his skull into the dirt beneath his head. That is graphic. And impressive. Barak shows up too late, but he can't say God didn't warn him. He leads the warriors, but the special glory goes to Deborah and Jael.

Then Deborah and Barak sing a victory hymn that poetically retells the story. This is the high point of a huge celebration party with lots of roasted sheep, wine, and Bollywood-style dancing. OK, the party isn't described in the Bible, but that's how it goes in my head. You can just feel the joy and triumph coming through.

And there was peace for forty years.

Living with Deborah

Both Sides Now

There are only two chapters about Deborah, and the second one retells the first, but in poetry.

The prose chapter is a well-constructed, complete story. We get the religious and historical setting, Deborah's and Barak's roles, God's instructions, battle strategy, and Sisera's death. It's a nice, tidy package.

The poetic chapter is dramatic and fun because it's a celebration song. This is when it gets personal, immediate, and full of interesting details. Deborah stops bandits plaguing travelers, tribes are shamed for skipping battle, and "the onrushing torrent, the torrent Kishon" washed away the enemy.

What I find most poignant in Deborah's song is a bit imagining Sisera's mother when he never comes home.

> Out of the window she peered,
>   the mother of Sisera gazed through the lattice:
> "Why is his chariot so long in coming?
>   Why do the hoofbeats of his chariots tarry?" (Jgs 5:26)

Deborah clearly sings this triumphantly, especially since the next lines are from the mother's maids saying that Sisera's probably just picking out the best slave girls and loot to bring home. For me it brings home the fact that Sisera is someone's son, just like all those other warriors. It makes all those people feel vividly alive for me. It's a touch, however chilling, that we don't often get.

These two versions are like reading the book and seeing the movie. Each has a slightly different attitude, while both communicate the truth. Scripture does this all the time. That's why Genesis has two versions of Adam's creation, and four Gospels tell Jesus' life story.

What can't be ignored in either version of this story is that it is God's story, first and foremost. Deborah, Barak, and Jael are important, but the storytellers are really talking about God's protection of his beloved people. In case we don't get it, right after Jael nails Sisera with that tent peg, we're told, "So on that day God subdued Jabin the king of Canaan before the sons of Israel." Bam. The victory is God's.

As much as I love looking at Deborah's story from several angles, I tend to resist this sort of view in my own life. The big picture of my own story is so often told from different points of view by my husband and children, family and friends. If I'm not too wedded to my own version, I can learn more about myself, good or bad. My life is enriched when I open myself up to community and allow myself to be known more fully.

Crushing It for God

Deborah's the whole package: legal counselor, prophetess, military commander, wife, and singer. But these only tell us the things she does, not who she is. Some of the prophets just will not shut up about how they're feeling or what's being done to them. Jeremiah wishes he'd never been born and is known as the weeping prophet. Elijah has to have an angel coax him back into action with a catered meal after he lies down under a tree saying, "I'm done. Take me now, Lord."

Deborah? She's kicking butt and taking names. We don't

know — or, frankly, care — how she restores order when bandits roam freely, what it does to her marriage to become a prophetess and judge, or what it's like to be a battlefield commander with Barak. She serves God without hesitation, without doubt, and with her whole heart.

Jael too, though not a prophet or judge, didn't mess around. We don't know why she breaks nearly every taboo in the book to get Sisera in a position where she can kill him. Women never invited men into their tents and — do we have to say it — it's terrible hospitality to kill guests. Especially don't kill the guest if he's an ally, because now we're in covenant-breaking territory. But Jael is all in.

Whatever God ordered up, these ladies got it done.

I love that the storytellers didn't try to clean things up. Women prophesying, leading armies, executing enemies — it's all on the table when you're telling God's story. If he gets messy, that's how we're gonna tell it. From their point of view, these unlikely heroes are just one more proof that only God could maneuver this whole crazy plan into working.

Women prophesying, leading armies, executing enemies — it's all on the table when you're telling God's story.

You can't lock God in a box. His ways are mysterious. God reads hearts, not genders or job descriptions. He knows who we are and what we can do. Our job is to cooperate by stepping out in faith and doing what he asks of us. Just wear your boots, because it might get messy.

Privileged to Collaborate

We've focused on woman-power, but let's look at Barak, the other major player in this story. He is respected enough to rally ten thousand warriors and lead them to a blowout victory. That's not the kind of guy who usually comes running when a woman orders, even if she is a judge and prophetess. But Barak respects

Deborah's authority enough to respond to her summons.

Deborah is literally using God's words, saying, "I will draw Sisera, the general of Jabin's army, to meet you by the river Kishon with his chariots and his troops; and I will give him into your hand."

But Barak hesitates, saying, "If you will go with me." That "if" changed the ultimate hero of the battle, with Jael getting the glory of Sisera's death. Why does Barak put conditions on his obedience? Is he afraid? Does he or do his troops need a tangible "talisman" of God's favor? Does he doubt God's power? We simply don't know. Again, this story is about God's victory, not individuals' internal journeys.

I get Barak. "Yes, but ... " seems to be one of my favorite phrases when God's desires come to me. No one's asking me to face down nine hundred weapons of mass destruction, but taking dinner to an ill neighbor down the street can feel just as daunting when I don't know her.

Sometimes, I'm afraid; sometimes, I'm doubting; and sometimes, I want control. "Sure thing, God, great idea — let me just add a wrinkle. If that doesn't work, then we'll go with your plan." God keeps shoving us out of our comfort zones in the hopes that someday we'll say yes and then shut up. Just so we can see, like Deborah and Jael, how amazing it can be when things get messy and God works them out.

Barak is included in a list of heroes of the faith in Hebrews 11 where Saint Paul says, "out of weakness they were made powerful, became strong in battle, and turned back foreign invaders." I take solace in the fact that God used Barak despite his weakness, whatever it was.

This is what I've got to remember. Every time I answer God's commands, I am rewarded with overflowing generosity. My life becomes richer, I become stronger in faith, and I know God a little more personally.

Also, Barak doesn't hold a grudge or blame people for his shortcomings. He's right there with Deborah singing that celebration hymn. That also encourages me to keep the right perspective and rejoice in God's victory no matter how imperfect my collaboration might be.

I still haven't gotten that victory party with roasted sheep and Bollywood dancing, but a girl can always hope!

Chapter IV

Samuel

Hope in a Desperate Hour

Samuel said, "Speak, for your servant hears." Then the Lord said to Samuel, "Behold, I am about to do a thing in Israel, at which the two ears of every one that hears it will tingle."

1 Samuel 3:10–11

What to Read

- 1 Samuel 1–28

The books of Samuel tell about an underdog who overcomes lowly origins and determined enemies to become the great king of Israel — David!

Hold on. Then why are these books named after Samuel? Because Samuel is the experienced mentor guiding our young hero, David, to become king. Samuel, the last of the judges, is a hands-on prophet, working behind the scenes to put David on the throne. We know this type from stories — Gandalf, Professor X, Mr. Miyagi. But Samuel's a real person, and there's a whole nation resting on his actions.

It's not easy. But Samuel never falters. He might ask questions. He might not understand why God wants something done. But he trusts in the Lord and follows his marching orders.

Samuel, Saul, and David are the big personalities in this

book, but I love the side stories that fill out the details: Hannah is accused of being sloshed while she's praying for a baby; the Philistines capture the Ark of the Covenant; and Eli has to deal with his terrible sons. These are all tales that give us perspective and make history come alive.

Quick Take on Samuel

Samuel is a kid living at the temple when he hears someone call his name in the middle of the night. Turns out it's the living God. Things are never the same after that for either Samuel or Israel.

Israel hadn't had a true prophet in decades. Samuel's the complete package — teacher, judge, and prophet. Times are good. Until Samuel gets old and appoints his sons as judges. They're so corrupt that the people tell Samuel they want a king "like all the nations."

Samuel's sure this is a bad idea: "Let me spell out all the crap your kings will put you through." No one's listening. Except God, who tells Samuel that he'll give the people just what they asked for. Uh-oh. Is this "be careful what you wish for" territory? He sends Samuel to find Saul and anoint him as Israel's first king.

God does take the people literally. He gives them a king who is just like the ones the other nations have: tall, good-looking, and strong. Also selfish, cowardly, foolish, paranoid, and greedy. He disobeys God, grabs all the good stuff for himself, and sets the people at each other's throats. Maybe the people should've looked more closely at those other nations before they asked. It's too late now. Samuel spends all his time trying to keep Saul in line. This is not working out.

Then God gives the people David. David is the king after God's own heart. Humble, accomplished, and dedicated to obeying the Lord. What more do you want? Well, you might want to have the first king gone before you anoint the second, but that's not how God rolls on this one. He tells Samuel that David's anointing will just be their little secret. David is fine with this (dedicated to obeying the Lord, after all). He even serves Saul as a musician after killing that pesky giant Goliath when no one else was up to the job.

You can't hide a big talent like David's, though. The people love him, but Saul's jealous and paranoid, remember? It's not long before he's trying to kill David. Soon David is living guerilla-style in the mountains, playing tag with Saul and his warriors. He gets a lot of chances to kill Saul, but never follows through because — you know — he's God's anointed. (I can't believe how obedient David is.)

Samuel dies, so Saul gets a witch to raise the prophet's ghost to give him advice. Huge sin alert! Samuel cannot believe what Saul just did, but sticks the landing, telling Saul before vanishing that the king will be dead by tomorrow.

Living with Samuel

Doing Things in God's Time, Not Ours

Adam and Eve eat from the forbidden tree of knowledge. Sarah and Abraham use her servant Hagar to get a son. Jacob steals his brother Esau's birthright, with their mom's help. (That one gets me every time.)

We love to force things to happen when we want them instead of waiting for God's timing.

We love to force things to happen when we want them instead of waiting for God's timing. That's not just in the Bible but all through human history. It's like a recipe for pain and suffering later.

1 Samuel, though, begins with the opposite. Hannah, a childless woman, struggles to accept God's timing. At the temple, Hannah vows that if God will give her a son, then she'll give that son back to him. She's swaying, crying, and her lips are moving soundlessly. No wonder Eli the priest thinks she's drunk. When she explains, he gives her God's blessing, and nine months later Samuel is born.

Samuel's name means "gift from God." When he is about

three, Hannah lives up to her part of the bargain. She takes him to live at the temple, where he will learn to be a priest. Hannah goes on to have five more children, but we know she misses little Samuel because she makes him a new robe every year. That's when you feel how much her obedience costs.

I suffered deep distress when waiting to conceive my own first child, so I feel Hannah's pain. She doesn't try to force the system by using a servant to have her child, which was totally legal and acceptable in those days. She takes it to God, persevering in prayer. She trusts. And she is blessed. After leaving Samuel at the temple, Hannah prays a beautiful song of praise for God's goodness to the weak, the hungry, the barren, and the needy.

That prayer (1 Sm 2:1–10) reminds us of a famous prayer by another woman who is blessed by God with a son: Mary. God's timing for Mary is just the opposite of what you'd expect. Early. Very early. In fact, she's a virgin. And suddenly, pregnant … at the same time. Mary's prayer, called the Magnificat (Lk 1:46–55), is just as full of trust and joy in God's goodness as Hannah's. That's pretty remarkable, considering most people might be worried sick.

I look at the complete trust of Hannah and Mary who offered their thanks by giving up their sons for the glory of God. It makes me think of when my daughters were little. I'd worry about their future, especially when the prayers of the faithful would pray "for an increase of priests and religious." I could just imagine my girls becoming cloistered nuns, and me never seeing them again. This was not a happy feeling. One day I was washing dishes, and this worry popped up. I remembered something a wise friend had said, "God doesn't have any grandchildren."

That sank deep. I got it. God would have a personal relationship with my children just the same as he did with me. Did I trust him to lead me, to want the best for me, to help me through tough times? Did I trust his plan for them to be as perfect as it has been for me? Whether I realized it at the time or not? Of course. And he would do the same for them.

Hannah and Mary suddenly came a little closer too. My trust is not as pure as theirs. My kids are grown. But I still have to trust in God's timing and not my own. That'll last until the day I die. If my faith can grow closer to Hannah's example, then I'll be content.

"Many Are Called but Few Are Chosen"

Jesus says this at the end of a parable in which one person after another turns down a wedding invitation; and, perhaps worse, those who do show up don't even care enough to put on decent clothes. It's not that God doesn't call them. It's that they turn him down. Samuel's story has vivid examples of that very problem.

Eli is the priest who trains Samuel. That makes it ironic that Eli's own sons are terrible priests. They eat the sacrifices meant for God, and they sleep with women at the temple. Eli hears the complaints, but only halfheartedly tries to discipline them.

When Samuel appoints his own sons to the priesthood, they start taking bribes. The result is that the people ask for a king instead. Oops. God says it isn't Samuel's fault, so that's a relief, at least.

Saul is given multiple do-overs, but he always does what he wants and gives Samuel a boatload of weak excuses. We know that doesn't turn out well for him or his family. Or for Israel, come to think of it.

God can always set things right in the end, but every time we turn him down or only go halfway, someone suffers. Am I one of those who turns aside, drifts like a leaf in the wind? Or will I go the whole way, even when it is brutally difficult? Where in my life am I saying "good enough," instead of "all for you, Lord"?

What would happen if we were all like Samuel, if everyone answered God's call? It would be a lot closer to heaven on earth.

God Doesn't Need Our Help

In case we think God is waiting around for our help, here's one of the funniest stories in the Bible. The Ark of the Covenant is captured during battle by the Philistines. Not knowing what else to do with it, they put it in the temple of their god Dagon. Because that's where gods go, right? In the morning, Dagon's statue is lying on the ground in front of the ark. Maybe it was an earthquake? Hmmm. No way to really tell. So they put Dagon back. The next morning, Dagon is right back at the foot of the ark, but with his head and hands broken off. Now does everyone get the message?

Just to rub it in, the city has a sudden infestation of mice. They're everywhere. But wait, there's more. Everyone gets a plague. Translations are uncertain — it is either tumors, boils, or hemorrhoids. No matter what, it hurts. The townspeople do what anyone would. They send the ark to a different town — twice. Where everything happens again.

Suddenly, the Philistines have got that good, old-time religion. The Hebrews' God is real, and he needs to be back home where he belongs. Problem solved.

No one needs to rescue the ark. God can get himself home. But in both of the books of Samuel, and the whole Bible, too, people are asked to carry out God's will. Samuel, for example, was as busy as a beaver judging and prophesying, crowning kings, correcting kings, replacing kings. So much to do with kings — which he never wanted in the first place. But he kept on doing what God asked.

So why does God use human help so much? It began as early as the garden of Eden, when "The Lord God took the man and put him in the garden of Eden to till it and keep it." That was before the animals were named, and Eve was created. Clearly man's cooperation in God's creation was part of the plan from the start. Why?

Two ideas come to mind. One is that we receive a good we wouldn't get otherwise. I have learned discipline and patience and a lot of other things from endeavors I've taken on for God.

There's also the joy of creation, of working hand-in-hand

with God. Often, of course, you get both in one package. (God's economical that way.)

In my own case, our parish's marriage retreat is an effort to prepare and present. By the time it is finished, I've been blessed by being part of the retreat and by seeing the attendees' sheer happiness. There's also a unique joy that comes from working with a team toward a common goal. If it's for God, then that's twice as good.

Why do I cooperate with God? There are a lot of possible reasons depending on the circumstances — love, serving others, possible benefit to myself, just because he asks. Am I always excited about God's jobs for me? I wish. Sometimes yes, sometimes no. But I try to cooperate with enthusiasm either way. And some of my rough edges are getting smoothed out with continued practice.

Chapter V

David

Rock Star, Hero, and Prophet

Saul said to his servants, "Provide for me a man who can play well, and bring him to me." One of the young men answered, "Behold, I have seen a son of Jesse the Bethlehemite, who is skilful in playing, a man of valor, a man of war, prudent in speech, and a man of good presence; and the Lord *is with him."*

1 Samuel 16:17–18

What to Read

David's life:

- 1 Samuel 16 through all of 2 Samuel, ending with 1 Kings 2:12
- 1 Chronicles 10:1—29:30

The two biggies connecting David's prophecies with Christ:

- Psalm 22 as a prophecy of Christ's Passion (Mk 15, Mt 27, Lk 23, Jn 19)
- Psalm 110, which Jesus quotes as a prophecy about the Messiah (Mt 22:41–46; Mk 12:35–37; Lk 20:4–44)

More of David's prophetic psalms:

- 2, 8, 16, 22, 34, 35, 40, 41, 68, 69, 109, 110

David? A prophet? Hardly! He's a doer — a lover, a fighter, a shepherd, a king. Prophets are the ones who guided David. But in Acts, we read "Being therefore a prophet, and knowing that God had sworn with an oath to him that he would set one of his descendants upon his throne, he foresaw and spoke of the resurrection of the Christ, that he was not abandoned to Hades, nor did his flesh see corruption." Peter was originally a fisherman, so can I trust him to have solid information when it comes to scriptural history?

It turns out Peter's on the mark. Believe it or not, songwriting — psalms! — is what gets David named a prophet. His soulful ballads bring King Saul back to his senses, and his joyful hymns make people dance in the streets. Right before David dies, we are told, "he who sang as none other sang in Israel. Through me the spirit of the Lord has spoken; his words are on my tongue."

Rock star, hero, and prophet of God, in one sweet package.

David lived so large that three thousand years later, it only takes a few words to make us think of key parts of his life. David and Goliath. David and Bathsheba. Even today his life is taught as an inspiration or cautionary tale. Let's round out the story.

Quick Take on David

When David's just a young shepherd, Samuel is sent by God to secretly anoint him as king. Secretly, because King Saul is still on the throne, although it's clear a replacement is needed. But David still has some growing up to do. When he brings his older brothers supplies during a big standoff between the Israelites and the Philistines, David steps up. He faces down Goliath with nothing but a sling, a stone, and the name of the Lord. Goliath went down hard. No wonder we love this kid.

David becomes Saul's favorite servant, singing when Saul has the blues and learning the military life. When everyone (and I mean everyone) loves David more than the king, Saul decides to kill him. David goes on the run, eluding and outsmarting the king and his army but refusing to hurt one hair on Saul's head.

That's just the kind of guy he is. After all, if God put this king in place, who is David to say it's a bad choice? He sticks with God's plan, however dangerous and confusing it seems. Brave, noble, and obedient to God — who's more kingly than David? No one, that's who.

Saul is killed in battle, and David becomes king by public acclaim. (Saul wasn't wrong to worry about his popularity.) David brings the Ark of the Covenant to Jerusalem and sets up the kingdom of Israel.

Now God makes a covenant with David that he and his descendants will rule Israel forever. The Messiah, meaning "the anointed one," will be a future king from David's line who will bring peace for everyone. This is the promise that Jesus will fulfill.

But that's just the first half of the story. Even the best of us can give in to the dark side. And that's what happens once David has it easy. Everyone else is off soldiering, but he's at home letting his eyes wander where they shouldn't. Bathsheba taking a bath on the next roof over is a temptation to adultery that David doesn't turn down. What follows is a classic noir tale of lust, betrayal, and calculated murder. I really can't believe this is the same David who was so upstanding and close to God.

David eventually makes things right with God, but it goes downhill from here. He's never going to be father of the year, and his family is about as dysfunctional as they come. They commit rape, incest, and murder, and begin a civil war. Worse yet, David does nothing to stop them, though he's angry and mournful about everyone's pain. Eventually David pulls it together, gets the kingdom and his family back in order, and names Solomon as king before he dies.

You know, I love David. And I get so mad at him. The one thing David never leaves you feeling is neutral. You're either for or against. That's why thinking about the psalms he wrote opens up a whole new look at this legendary king. We get to see the inner David as he opens up to God in song.

Quick Take on Psalms

David wrote about half of the psalms, including some of the best known, with imagery that takes us right into his deepest feelings. In a way, those psalms are like a spiritual memoir, recording moments from his life.

A world of experience and emotion are in this book. The psalmists don't hold back. They praise God, complain to him, thank him, and ask for their deepest desires. Which means that the psalms apply to everything we face every day: joy, sorrow, disillusionment, success, and failure.

The 150 psalms in the Bible were written over a 750-year period. That's a big best-seller list coming our way. The psalms have been part of Jewish liturgy since they were invented, and we inherited them in our Catholic liturgy. And, of course, we all know the psalms. They've been prayed personally by people for that whole time — thousands of years. That stuff's too good to leave in church, because it's also personal. In one handy book, we have sublime praise, heartbreaking lamentation, and profound worship.

What's easy to forget is that all these individual psalms had to be collected and organized to become the book we use today. They are sorted into five "books," which follow a loose telling of the kingdom of David, beginning with his sufferings, rise, and decline, and ending with the exile to Babylon, return to Israel, and hope for God's fulfillment of the Davidic covenant in the coming of the Messiah. So that means that centuries before Jesus, the psalms were looked at as being about the Messiah.

I never thought about someone organizing the psalms, much less with a plan in mind. I just read them all as individual pieces. That explains why our ancient editor placed David's psalms throughout those five books, instead of huddled together chronologically. Some tell one part of the story, some tell another — some even prophesy about the Messiah.

Some of David's psalms are quoted specifically in the New Testament as messianic prophecy fulfilled by Jesus. Reading them now with what we know of Jesus' life, some of those scenes eerily call up the Passion and crucifixion. Jesus also often quotes psalms when describing himself and his Messianic mission. It turns out when David is singing, God's words really are on his tongue.

Living with David and the Psalms

Multitasking — Prophecy That Speaks to the Soul

Psalms is a prophetic book that you (usually) don't have to struggle to understand or get your arms around. Whatever's happening in your life, the psalms are there with the perfect way to express it to God … and to ourselves as we learn who we are through our experiences.

This is the prayer book that the Holy Spirit has inspired. Jesus prayed the psalms during his life as a devout Jew — that's how he knows them so well.

Check out Psalm 22. I just about dropped my Bible the first time I was flipping through psalms and read, "My God, my God, why have you abandoned me?"

Jesus knew Psalm 22. He didn't speak randomly when he quoted the first lines from the cross. He alerted listening Jews that Psalm 22, which they knew well, was coming alive at that moment. He also spoke for everyone who ever feels abandoned by God. A lot of what Jesus says can be taken on many levels, and that definitely applies to the psalms as well.

Look at Psalm 22, verse 14:

> I am poured out like water,
>   and all my bones are out of joint;
> my heart is like wax,
>   it is melted within my breast.

I know that moment. Not in the same way David does; not like Jesus does, either. But who hasn't had that feeling of shock, of dislocation, of fear, and despair? We all know that moment.

This is how God uses the Bible to speak to us personally. That bit of text that catches our eye, and our heart, with the experience we know so well down to our very core. Joy, sorrow, shock, exultation. Reading these psalms, knowing David's life and his relationship with God, turns the psalms into a school. They are not only a school of prayer, but an education of how to live our lives talking to God and learning to love him better.

This is how God uses the Bible to speak to us personally.

Do I open myself to God personally when I am reading the psalms? Do I take it to the level of what is happening in my life at this time, at this moment? Just a bit of daily Bible reading with that intention can make a huge difference in my life.

Double, Triple, Quadruple Meanings

Maybe no other prophet demonstrates so well that God will use anything and everything to get his message across. David does say that he knows God uses his mouth, but that is at the end of his life, after he's had time to meditate on things. I wonder whether much of the time David is just doing what songwriters and men of God do — sharing his inner feelings in his songs and offering them to God.

Do the prophets always know they are having a vision of the future aside from the situation they're stuck in at the moment? That's a mixed bag — sometimes maybe yes, but I'd bet more often probably not. What we see time and again is the prophets wrestling with their particular circumstances, not worrying about an unforeseeable future. Even in cases such as Isaiah and Jeremiah, where they were reporting visions of the future, it was of a fairly immediate future that mattered specifically to their own times.

It turns out, though, that those prophecies aren't limited to only their times. The prophecies could often be read by looking backward or into several layers of meaning. The prophets often say more than they know. They are talking about their own moment in time without knowing that God will also use their words to have significance in the future. In fact, Jesus points this out to the disciples on the road to Emmaus, one of my favorite Resurrection stories. There are twenty-five "Messianic psalms" that are part of this tradition.

That's why we have to continually try to offer the best of ourselves to God. Even when it doesn't make sense, even when it doesn't seem to matter … when we do God's will, then we are available to be his conduit to more than the immediate moment. We just might be the instrument that he can use to work in the world both now and in the future. Like David, we often have no way of knowing this, or even of imagining how it might work. But we can do our best and trust God to use us in ways we can't imagine in the moment.

Seeking God from the Heart

Here's the thing that we know David couldn't imagine. The Messiah has come, and his followers are still praising and complaining and laughing and wrestling with God. We're still using David's words, several thousand years after he sang and prayed and prophesied. And God is using those same words to comfort, guide, answer, and love us. Especially to love us.

David isn't thinking about his legacy when he sings. He's talking to the living God, wanting to love and trust him more. David is wrestling through his life, for good and ill. He knows that any life without God in the center is empty and lonely and goes terribly wrong sooner or later. More importantly, he also knows that a life guided by God, open to his love and mercy, will be better than anything he could imagine. In Psalm 30, he sings:

> You have turned my mourning into dancing;
>   you have loosed my sackcloth
>   and clothed me with gladness,
> that my soul may praise you and not be silent.

> O Lord my God, I will give thanks to you for ever.
> (vv. 11–12)

No matter what you and the psalmist are praying about, every psalm includes one thing — praise of God. Because in the end, that's where life takes us, or should. Whatever you've got to say to God, Psalms got there first, and probably more than once.

Chapter VI

Nathan

Speaking Truth to Power

In accordance with all these words, and in accordance with all this vision, Nathan spoke to David.

2 Samuel 7:17

What to Read

- 2 Samuel 7:1–29
- 2 Samuel 11; 12:1–25
- 1 Kings 1

We see Nathan only three times, on occasions when he's delivering God's messages to David. There's no adventure, no back story, no lamenting or showboating; that's for the other prophets. Nathan is quick and efficient. This makes it sound as if he's only a delivery boy; but Nathan's definitely more than that, especially since David and Bathsheba name their second son after him. That sounds more like a family friend.

Nathan's got integrity and guts. Which is a good thing, because every time he shows up, David gets a reversal on the way he thinks things are going. Even when the message is straight from God, that doesn't usually stop the rich and powerful from taking it out on the messenger (just ask Jeremiah). But the way Nathan approaches each of these moments shows us he's smart and able to read a situation. Every time, David takes it the right way. That also shows his trust in Nathan and in God.

Nathan's prophetic communications are three defining moments in David's life and, more importantly, in the kingship of Israel and God's covenant with his Chosen People.

Quick Take on Nathan

King David's sitting pretty in his palace, but he doesn't like to think of God's ark stuck in a tent. It deserves the most beautiful temple around, and David's gonna build it. Nathan loves this plan and gives David the go-ahead.

God says thanks, but no thanks. Nathan says that instead, God will build David a "house," meaning a royal dynasty. It will last forever, and God will always support it as a loving father. No one saw that coming! This is one of the most ancient of the Messianic prophecies — the Savior will be of the house of David. David is blown away, and who wouldn't be? His prayer of thanks is touching, reminding us that he wrote some of the most moving psalms.

A few war campaigns later, David's on his rooftop when he catches sight of a gorgeous woman bathing. She's Bathsheba, the wife of army officer Uriah the Hittite who, unlike David, is off at the wars where all fighting men should be. David has her brought to him. It's a one-night stand, and he doesn't see Bathsheba again until he gets a note saying she's pregnant. C'mon David, you're better than this. Aren't you?

David orders Uriah home so he'll sleep with Bathsheba and think the baby is his. Uriah says that if his soldiers can't visit their wives, he won't visit his, either. By this time we're wishing he was king instead of David. So David sends him back to the war with a note to the general, who makes sure Uriah dies in battle. David marries Bathsheba as soon as she is done with her seven-day mourning period. No time to waste — she'll be showing soon. Wow: lust, murder, seduction, and turning from God. We're in a very dark place now.

God sends Nathan to David, and Nathan asks the king to "judge a case." He tells the story of a poor man who had nothing but a little pet lamb. It was cooked up for a guest by a rich man who selfishly chose not to kill his own sheep. David, furious, says the rich man deserves death. Nathan says to David, "You are the man!" See, you can't hide from God, who is furious too — as Nathan expresses at length and in detail. David admits his sin, repents, and seeks absolution. God forgives him, but the consequences of David's actions will ripple through the royal family, beginning with the death of the child he conceived with Bathsheba.

Nathan appears again when David is close to death. David's oldest son, Adonijah, jumps the gun and has himself publicly proclaimed as king. Nathan works with Bathsheba to gently awaken David to the situation and crown the rightful heir. Meet King Solomon.

Living with Nathan

Who's Running This Show?

The thing that always impresses me about Nathan is how fearless he is when conveying God's words. Nobody wants to tell someone he's gotta give up his dreams, especially when you just gave him a thumbs-up on that new temple yesterday. Of course, telling David "no" is only going to disappoint him for as long as it takes to get to the part about God's special covenant with him. I can just see Nathan's huge grin when he gets to that part of "thus sayeth the Lord."

The thing that always impresses me about Nathan is how fearless he is when conveying God's words.

God reminds both of them that he's got a plan for David's life, and a plan for human history. We aren't told why God doesn't want a temple now, or why David isn't the right person to build it. That's not important. What's important is what David does with the info. He's trusting and grateful, humbly giving thanks for the blessings that will benefit not only him, but also, all of Israel.

This makes me think two things. First, do I believe God has a plan for my life? In our post-Christian secular world, that can be a hard thing to relate to. What is coincidence and what isn't? What about free will — where do the choices we make come into the picture?

Second, if God says no to a cherished dream, how do I take it? Am I willing? Do I fight it? I'm no David, and when God denies a dream I usually don't get a long, detailed explanation of the much better blessing that will come instead.

If I hadn't dealt with this sort of thing in my life, these hard questions might just derail me. I used to be an agnostic, always wondering how people knew God existed. When my husband and I couldn't sell our house, I decided to ask God to prove his existence by getting us a new house. After a year, though, somehow my attitude had changed. I told God that I would believe in him without any proof and that he was off the hook for a new house. The very next day things started happening, and within one month we were in a wonderful new house.

It took a huge string of "coincidences," but I knew what it meant. God cared about me personally, enough to change my heart *and* give me a new house. He'd done what was needed so that I'd pay attention when he took action.

The key to being like Nathan — and David — is a personal relationship with God. We only have to be willing to ask for it. And, of course, to pay attention!

"You Are the Man!"

I feel a minute of ringing silence after Nathan thunders these words. David has to be stunned as he's connecting the dots.

It's never easy pointing out what a powerful person has done wrong. They like to chop first, think later. Who knows what David might do? Remember what Pharaoh had done to Moses and the Hebrews?

Nathan cannot have looked forward to this meeting, but he was both fearless and subtle. He applies the one-two punch of a parable, followed by the Lord's devastatingly direct message. Telling the parable gets David's attention, activates his sense of justice, and then pulls the rug out from under him. However Nathan feels about finding out that David is an adulterer and cold-blooded murderer, his goal is noble. God and Nathan want to restore David as the righteous leader he once was. And that can't happen if David doesn't admit his actions and repent.

It works. David folds faster than Superman on laundry day. He doesn't get a chance to do more than admit his guilt before Nathan tells him that God has already forgiven his sin. This makes me remember Jesus' parable (Lk 15:11–32) in which the prodigal son doesn't even have time to finish his rehearsed apology before his father cuts him off with a new wardrobe and "welcome home" party plans. The point is, God's great mercy is always waiting for us.

Just like most people, I dread bringing up hard truths, and I love it even less when a friend is involved. But if I don't care enough to try to help a friend know the truth, what kind of friend am I? Keeping silent makes me partially responsible for the consequences. If I don't say anything, am I keeping them from experiencing God's mercy? What about when I'm "David" and a friend approaches me with an unwelcome hard truth? Can I follow David's model of acceptance and repentance?

What helps is keeping in mind that the goal is to help restore the ability to see the truth without blinders on, no matter what may have been done. That is the first step to solving any problem.

Taking Matters into Your Own Hands

When Adonijah has himself made king, we get a new look at Nathan in action. For one thing, this is the only time when we are not told that "the Lord sent Nathan" and "thus sayeth the Lord." Nope. Nathan is on his own, playing it cool, showing the experience of a lifetime of royal service. He prompts Bathsheba to ask David a few simple questions that alert him that Solomon's about to be edged out. Then Nathan does the same from a slightly different angle.

In this case, sensitivity is especially important — the author drops in a pointed comment noting that David hadn't ever disciplined Adonijah. No wonder Adonijah thinks he can just take what he wants. That's not just interesting backstory; it's also part of a lifelong pattern for David's children. One of his sons rapes his own half-sister; another son takes revenge by killing the rapist; and a third son begins a rebellion to take over the kingdom. All while David stands aside and doesn't act. Now this entitled son is grabbing power. Hey, parenting matters, David!

A blunt approach might have led to David feeling defensive or falling into old patterns of allowing Adonijah what he wanted. There is a lot to be said for asking questions, listening, and letting people think things through for themselves. It allows the person the dignity of having their own opinions respected, which is something that is often not accorded these days to someone as old as David.

I like that we have this example of Nathan working under his own steam. We see Bathsheba's trust in Nathan's plan, David's return to kingly action, and Nathan using all his skills on behalf of what's right. Nathan doesn't need divine instructions in this case. It's pretty obvious that there's going to be a disaster if he doesn't step in.

This is how we have to be. We're here to live our ordinary lives the best way we can. Our human efforts on behalf of those we love, to do what's right, and in service of God are the threads woven together into the tapestry of God's big plan. He put us here to use our own judgment and skills. And that is comforting.

Chapter VII

Elijah

Nuking the Pagans

[Elijah said] "And you call on the name of your god and I will call on the name of the Lord*; and the God who answers by fire, he is God." And all the people answered, "It is well spoken." And [the prophets of Baal] took the bull which was given them, and they prepared it, and called on the name of Baal from morning until noon, saying, "O Baal, answer us!" But there was no voice, and no one answered. And they limped about the altar which they had made. And at noon Elijah mocked them, saying, "Cry aloud, for he is a god; either he is musing, or he has gone aside, or he is on a journey, or perhaps he is asleep and must be awakened."*

1 Kings 18:24, 26–27

What to Read

- 1 Kings 17–19, 2 Kings 1–2

Do we even have to ask what happens next? Elijah has the altar to the Lord drenched with water three times. And then he calls down a firestorm that turns the sacrifice to ashes and evaporates all the water. This is even better when you know that Baal is the Canaanite god of rain, thunder, lightning, and dew.

1 Kings starts off with King David's final days and King Solomon's grand kingdom. After that things go downhill, in an

endless list of kings' political and religious schisms. For every good king, there are ten going from bad to worse: "But [insert king's name here] did what was evil in the Lord's sight, more than any of his predecessors." You know there's no way that's turning out OK.

I'm not gonna lie. Reading this is a snoozefest until Elijah drops on the scene. Before we know it he's calling down fire from heaven, multiplying food, controlling weather, and raising the dead. All in God's name. Sound familiar? That's why when Jesus asks his disciples who people say he is, some report he's said to be Elijah the prophet. They recognize a miracle-working pattern when they see one.

Settle in with some popcorn. This is one miraculous show.

Quick Take on Elijah

Israel's king, Ahab, marries pagan princess Jezebel and makes the worship of her god, Baal, the new state religion. This is the most in-your-face evil any king of Israel has done yet. You know that's not going unanswered.

The first thing God does is declare a drought. Since Baal is the god of fertility, weather, rain, wind, and seasons, this is an obvious throwdown. God's extra-faithful prophet Elijah carries that message to Ahab and then goes on the lam, per God's orders. He's fed by ravens in the wilderness until the water runs out; then God sends him to a widow in Sidon. (That's Jezebel's home country. Nothing like hiding out right under her nose.) When Elijah arrives, the widow doesn't have enough food to keep even her own family alive. Elijah tells her that God will make sure the flour and oil don't run out until the drought is broken. Of course, he's right. There's always just enough for the next meal — for three years. When the widow's son dies, Elijah brings him back to life. Just another day in the life of the biggest miracle-working prophet in the Old Testament. Elijah's whole story is full of "firsts in Scripture," but the resurrection scene is one of the most impressive.

After three years, God's ready to stop the drought, so Elijah goes back to Ahab for the big showdown. It's 850 pagan prophets on Baal's side versus Elijah alone on God's team, with all the people watching from the sidelines. This is the spectacle to end all spectacles. We know the score: God 1–Baal 0. The people get the message and put Baal's prophets to the sword. Then, and only then, God ends the drought. (Get it, Ahab? You totally put your money on the wrong god.)

Now that he's cleaned house, Elijah gets a big award and is honored for the rest of his days. Right?

No such luck. Did I mention Jezebel is a truly evil queen? The very next day, she vows to give Elijah just what he gave to Baal's priests. Elijah gets out of town again — this time it's his own idea — and winds up in the desert sitting under a bush saying, "Take me now, Lord. I'm done." No way. An angel brings food and water and keeps pushing him until he eats every crumb. He's still got a journey to take, says the angel. So Elijah walks forty days and forty nights (Catch that? It's a very important biblical number meaning a long time) to a mountain, where he settles down in a cave.

God asks why he's in the cave, and Elijah says that he's been to hell and back for God with nothing to show for it but death threats. We get it, Elijah! God does, too. He tells the prophet to go stand on the mountain, because the Lord will pass by. A huge wind is ripping the mountain apart, but that's not the Lord. An earthquake happens. Not the Lord either. A fire happens. Still not the Lord. Where is he, anyway? Then there is a still, small voice. Oh, there he is. God tells Elijah to go anoint a new king of Israel, and pick up Elisha as a prophet apprentice. And by the way, there are still seven thousand Israelites who have not worshiped Baal, so Elijah's work hasn't been for nothing. Woohoo!

Elijah sets off and recruits Elisha, whom he comes across plowing with oxen. Elisha's excited, just stopping long enough to say goodbye to his parents, burn his plow, and slaughter his oxen for a farewell feast. There's no turning back now. And Elijah's not alone any more.

Back at the palace, Ahab's throwing a tantrum because his neighbor Naboth has a sweet vineyard that he won't sell. Jezebel has Naboth stoned to death and gives the vineyard to her sweetie. Who says you can't be a good wife and an evil queen at the same time? Elijah shows up — again — with God's message of a horrible death penalty for the murder. Ahab, always more sensitive than his wife, actually repents now with ashes, sackcloth, fasting, the whole nine yards. God knows he's sincere, so he pushes off punishment to the next generation. It is tough to be a royal heir these days.

After one more little side-quest (to school Ahab's son, the new king), it's time for Elijah to go to heaven. He parts the Jordan River with his rolled-up cloak so he and Elisha can walk to the rendezvous point. He works those mind-blowing miracles until the very end. Do we love this guy or what? A flaming chariot and flaming horses take him up to heaven in a whirlwind. That's right, Elijah doesn't die. In the most flamboyant way possible, we see death is not the end. God uses Elijah even in his last moments to send yet another message about divine reality. It's the perfect send-off for the greatest miracle worker in the Old Testament.

In the most flamboyant way possible, we see death is not the end.

Living with Elijah

"Ask Yourself One Question: 'Do I Feel Lucky?' Well, Do You, Baal?"

I love Elijah's style, especially at the big showdown with Baal's prophets. He's zinging everyone about their lame god while showing the real God's power. That attitude comes only when you believe in the miraculous, only when you've got ultimate trust in God. After all, the point of a miracle isn't just to show off, though that can be a fun side effect.

A miracle is a special work of God, outside of the laws of

nature, which reveals something about God's character or purposes. And a miracle is usually for a specific reason; in this case, clearly a demonstration for the people so they'd go back to worshiping the real God instead of a fake one. It's fair to say that the people probably also begin taking Elijah's divine authority seriously.

What does it take to be as supremely confident as Elijah? Setting up test conditions that go against any normal chance of winning makes it clear that if this works, it's going to be because of God, not Elijah. So that must mean Elijah has perfect trust in God.

Who do I "perfectly" trust? Who will never betray me? I've never thought about this question before now, but I realize it is a very short list — a few close family members and friends. Deep-down "take a bullet for you" trust is rare. The key to knowing who is on that list is how well I know the person and how many times we've come through for each other.

If God's making that list, where do I fall on it? I don't like thinking about that as much, because I can think of times when I turned him down or thought something could wait until later and just never got back to it.

I know who I am, but I have to wonder who I could be. Can I believe implicitly in the miraculous, and obey when it doesn't make sense? Do I have the wholehearted commitment, single-minded dedication, and steadfast obedience to be as fearless as Elijah? If I hold Elijah's example in front of me, could there be, someday, fire flashing from heaven?

Why So Sad, Elijah?

After Baal's prophets fail the test, Queen Jezebel is out for Elijah's blood — literally.

It's a huge about-face to see Elijah hiding under the bush wanting to die. Is this the fearless hero who's been taunting pagan gods? What is going on?

We see point-blank "Then [Elijah] was afraid, and he arose

and went for his life." Later, the Lord asks twice why Elijah is on the mountain, and both times Elijah says that everyone else is dead, the altars are destroyed, and "I, even I only, am left; and they seek my life." He's afraid and alone.

I love this moment under the bush when we see God's personal relationship with Elijah. He feeds him, makes sure he's cleaned his plate (twice), and sends him on an extended trek to a cave in a mountain in the middle of nowhere. Now that he's fed and safe and no one's going to bother them, God settles in for a chat. And the first thing he asks is, "What are you doing here, Elijah?"

This is when Elijah pours his heart out to God, and God does something odd. Instead of directly answering, he has Elijah go outside and "stand upon the mount before the Lord." We've seen God's fire blast the altar, but none of those big signs of power comes on the mountain. He's the still, small voice you hear deep in your heart.

Look at the power and surety of Elijah's faith. Yet even he still has to learn that God is not in the earthquake or the fire. Every small moment is still a moment with more to learn. That's when God brings us closer to himself. He deals intimately with Elijah on the mountain, discussing his thoughts and behavior, and assuring him that he's not alone. The personal moments here with God seem to help strengthen Elijah for the rest of his tasks.

We will never be able to fully grasp who God is. God is mysterious and unfathomable. But little by little we can learn more than we knew before, and always through personal relationship just like we see here. I'm comforted to see this great miracle worker struggling just like I do when nothing is going my way. My faith may not always be strong, but God always makes the first move, doing whatever it takes to get my attention. The next move is up to me. When that still, small voice comes, how do I respond?

You Came from Where?

Remember that widow with whom Elijah hides out during the

drought? Widows got no social assistance back in those days. If you aren't part of a household with a working man, you'll likely starve. That's just what this widow and her young son are about to do when Elijah shows up at her door. Not only is this a strange male visitor, but obviously one who worships that weird, foreign God (a.k.a not Baal), because she spots it right off, saying, "As the LORD your God lives, I have nothing baked."

I always think of this as God providing for Elijah. But from the widow's point of view, a strange, foreign God sends her a lifeline in hard times. We're told that she will have enough to eat for a long time. Her troubles are over! Then her son dies. Not only is she suffering what any mother would, but any hope is gone for a time when her son will eventually provide for them. She tells Elijah it's all his fault, him and his dumb God. Elijah takes the child from her and goes to his room, begging God to restore the child to life.

And he does. Deep in the heart of Baal-worshiping Sidon, we get the first resurrection in the Bible.

Smack-dab in the middle of Elijah's battle to make Israel pure again, we see that God cares about every human, not just the Chosen People. We're not supposed to breeze past this story thinking, "Oh, that's nice." It is told at considerable length to make sure we stop and pay attention. So what's the point?

There's hardly a more unlikely time and place for this astounding display of God's power than a poor widow's upstairs room with no audience. Maybe this is partly why Elijah is so confident when he's got to pull down that fire against Baal later.

Does this leave the widow as a believer inserted in Sidon? She says to Elijah, "Now I know that you are a man of God, and that the word of the Lord in your mouth is truth." God uses Elijah to make her path straight and maybe to leave a witness of his mercy and love planted in Sidon.

Elijah hides out to stay alive, but his presence blesses the widow. At the same time, working those miracles on her behalf surely furthers his trust in God. God often uses surprising sources for his purposes. When I think I'm helping someone else, am I really the one who is getting a blessing? When I resist doing God's will, am I turning down some good that God has planned for me but that I can't possibly imagine?

Chapter VIII

Elisha

A People Person

Then Elisha prayed, and said, "O Lord, *I pray thee, open his eyes that he may see."*

2 Kings 6:17

What to Read

- 1 Kings 19:16–21
- 2 Kings 2–9; 13:14–21

Elisha's tricky for me to keep track of. First off, his name is practically identical to his master Elijah's. Second, he does a lot of the same sorts of miracles. He actually does a ton more of them, but if you've ever had to take over for a popular boss and had a hard time getting noticed, you know what I'm talking about.

But Elisha's not a copycat, and the people know it. Elijah burns away idolatry so people can worship the true God, while Elisha demonstrates God's compassion, healing, and grace. The people need to know the powerful love of the God they've been away from for so long. Elisha opens their eyes so they can see.

Elisha's different in another way, too. No desert bushes or lonely mountain caves for him. He's a people person, at least as much as a gruff prophet can be. You'll find him with a crowd of other prophets, staying with friends every time he's in town; and even when he's in a hut by himself, he's not really alone. He's got a servant, Gehazi, who's like a comic sidekick.

These stories are packed with details about little servant girls, woodcutters, and lots of other ordinary people who discover that God is present in their lives even when they can't see him.

Quick Take on Elisha

Elisha witnesses Elijah being swept up to heaven in a fiery chariot. But before he goes, Elisha asks for a double portion of his spirit and gets it! Pow — next thing we know, he's splitting Jordan's waters, purifying bad water and poisoned stew, multiplying oil and bread, and raising a child from the dead. He's the real deal.

Elisha's also continually advising and prophesying to a series of kings, the way you do when you're a prophet in Israel. In the process, he finishes up the to-do list God gave Elijah in the cave by anointing Hazael as king of Aram and Jehu as king of Israel.

One of the stories about Elisha is hard for us moderns to take. A group of boys is making fun of him. Elisha calls down God's curse on them, and two bears come out of the woods and attack forty-two of them. Who's gonna tease one of God's prophets now?

Usually, though, Elisha shows unexpected mercy. Aramean general Naaman has a serious case of leprosy. Luckily, he gets word of Elisha's healing powers. He's outraged by the ridiculously simple cure Elisha prescribes. Then he tries it, and it works! Nobody's fool, Naaman realizes that this God is legit, and instantly converts.

So it goes with story after story, some funny, some poignant, but all showing God's power and goodness. Last of all, because even death's not stopping this guy, touching Elisha's corpse brings a man back to life, the first and only time *that* happens in the Old Testament.

Living with Elisha

Forty-Two Very Bad Boys and Two Hungry Bears

"He went up from there to Bethel; and while he was going up on the way, some small boys came out of the city and jeered at him, saying, "Go up, you baldhead! Go up, you baldhead!" And he turned around, and when he saw them, he cursed them in the name of the Lord. And two she-bears came out of the woods and tore forty-two of the boys."

Hey, I'm all for God sticking up for his prophet, but wild animals tearing apart forty-two little kids is a bit much even for me. And it seems inconsistent with Elisha's other actions. Then I found out that the translation above is super inaccurate. I can say that because this incident troubled me so much that I spent way too much time looking into vocabulary words. Anything to help dig the Lord out of this bad reputation, though.

It turns out that the Hebrew word *na'ar* translated as "small boys" often means "young men" of at least seventeen years old, certainly between twelve and thirty.* Bethel was one of the two centers in Israel for worshiping idols, so they were probably pagans. What about that smarty-pants jeering, "Go up, baldy"? Elisha was coming from Elijah's being borne away to heaven. People often shaved their heads in mourning, so Elisha's bald head may have been a result of losing his "father," as he called Elijah. The local prophets had sent fifty men seeking Elijah for three days in case Elijah had been left somewhere on earth. (They came up empty. When God takes a prophet to heaven, he stays taken.) So we see that people were having a hard time believing this event.

Now the story reads like this: At least forty-two young, pagan men got together to taunt the mourning Elisha and his God

---

* Trent Horn, *Hard Sayings: A Catholic Approach to Answering Bible Difficulties* (San Diego: Catholic Answers Press, 2016) 301. Also: Walter C. Kaiser Jr., Peter H. Davids, F. F. Bruce, and Manfred Brauch, *Hard Sayings of the Bible* (Westmont, Illinois: IVP Academic, 1996).

by saying that if he is really a prophet then he'll "go up" like Elijah did. Now I'm kind of worried about Elisha's safety. What are these guys gonna do? Then Elisha lays God's curse on them. Now this sounds like Elijah's disciple — sticking up for God's honor against pagan believers. Notice that God is the one deciding how to fulfill it. Suddenly, the story seems a bit more fair. And people are definitely going to take Elisha seriously now that they see the true God is backing him up.

Translation, translation, context, context. Words can have a lot of meanings, and those meanings can change. Sometimes a word makes all the difference. We've all been getting a good education lately in source checking, thanks to social media. Bible translation can be just as challenging. If something seems weird, dig deeper! There are plenty of commentaries covering every question you can come up with. And don't just pick one. Check several against each other to see what holds water, and look to the Church, the early Church Fathers, and the saints for reliable spiritual insight.

If something seems weird, dig deeper!

Go Jump in a River!

The story of Naaman's healing from leprosy is the story of God revealed through a little girl, servants, and a prophet who won't accept any reward — the humble and small. Sound familiar?

It all begins with Naaman's wife's servant, a young captive Israelite girl who knows Elisha can cure Naaman. Naaman's got nothing to lose except his leprosy. With a full entourage and riches on display, he finds his way to the legendary prophet's house.

Elisha doesn't even bother to come to the door. He sends a message that if Naaman washes seven times in the Jordan River, he will be both cured and cleansed. Nice — healing inside and out! But Naaman's furious. No prayers? No dramatic hand-waving? No personal appearance from Elisha? No important river to wash in? No thanks!

Naaman's servants point out that he'd try wackier things if the guys back home prescribed them. It's delightful to see the powerful, proud Naaman reduced to humbly doing as he's told without understanding any of the reasons why. To give Naaman credit, when the cure works, he's one hundred percent on board. He even asks permission to load up two boxes of earth so he can worship the true God back home in Aram.

I am a little ashamed to say how well I understand Naaman. I'm a contrarian and dig in my heels when things aren't being done just the way I think they should. Proud? Self-willed? Know-it-all? Yes, yes, and yes. And I always wind up eating humble pie. Always. But there's hope. Like Naaman, I know the delight of encountering the living God and discovering there is nothing sweeter than him. That definitely makes learning obedience easier, because it is for God, who loves me better than I love myself.

I'm slowly figuring out that when God wants something, there's always a good reason, even when I don't see it. What will it take before I just do things his way without arguing first? I have to practice wrestling with my pride and expectations in the small daily things to cooperate with God; but gradually, I am getting better at doing things his way before my own.

Thinking Outside the Box

One of my favorite Elisha stories has him giving sight, striking blind, and giving sight again. He's the only one with clear vision, and it leads him to be completely countercultural.

The Arameans have a problem. Elisha gets divine tips about their battle plans, which he passes along to the Israelite king. The enemy knows about Elisha. There's no time for subtle stuff. So they surround his location with their entire army. Gehazi freaks out, but Elisha's prayer lets him see that God's invisible army is protecting them. Then Elisha singlehandedly captures the army by asking God to strike them blind while he leads them to the Israelite king. When Elisha has God restore their sight, it's their turn to freak out. He reminds the Israelite king that you don't kill captives, and makes sure they get a nice meal before they go home. Who says you can't combine humor and hospitality?

I love this creative problem-solving, especially when you remember that the normal tactic was just to annihilate the enemy and be done with it. Elisha goes to a lot of trouble to neutralize the enemy while making sure they all get home OK. As a result, we are told, the Arameans stopped raiding. I bet. That would be enough to make me stay home for a very long time.

This is another way of seeing below the surface, which Elisha does so well. His unconventional solution and willingness to take a chance both come from trusting God. I don't have Elisha's sight, but in what do I put my faith? Am I willing to take a big chance for God and faith even when it goes against the commonly accepted customs of my day? When I insist that baptism cleanses us of sin even though we can't see it, the secular world doesn't believe. When I agree with the Church that marriage between a man and a woman is the only sort that satisfies both natural law and God's law, the secular world calls me intolerant.

To be fair, I've still got a lot of those moments myself. When I don't trust, when I don't stand up, when I have to be hit with a holy two-by-four … then I am more like Gehazi than Elisha, and a lot like the secular world I'm supposed to be helping look below the surface.

Chapter IX

Isaiah

The Big Book of Prophecy

And I heard the voice of the Lord saying, "Whom shall I send, and who will go for us?" Then I said, "Here am I! Send me."

Isaiah 6:8

What to Read

The easiest place to read Isaiah is in the liturgy of the Church (a.k.a. the Mass readings, when the pairings with the Gospels help shed light on how Isaiah's text shows us the truth about Jesus).

Just for fun, flip back and forth to find familiar Scripture that you didn't know originated in Isaiah. This is just a small sampling, but it will give you the idea.

- Isaiah 7:14 — Virgin with child (Mt 1:23)
- Isaiah 9:1 — A light in darkness (Mt 4:16)
- Isaiah 11:1–2 — The gifts of the Holy Spirit (*Catechism of the Catholic Church* 1831)
- Isaiah 40:3–5 — Voice in wilderness (Mt 3:1–3, Mk 1:2–3, Lk 3:4–5, Jn 1:23)
- Isaiah 42:1–4 — Behold my servant (Mt 12:15–21)
- Isaiah 42:6–7 — A light for the Gentiles (Mt 11:2–5, Lk 2:32)
- Isaiah 53:12 — Numbered with transgressors (Lk

22:37)
- Isaiah 54:13 — All be taught of God (Jn 6:45)

Meet the big man, the prophet Isaiah. The most major among Israel's prophets, beloved by Jews and Christians alike.

I'm not gonna lie. This isn't a book to cuddle up with for a good read. There are a few historical bits, but most of the sixty-six chapters (yep, it's a long one) are full of prophecy about politics and places that are long gone.

Why do we even care? Let's start with this little tidbit. Jesus opened his public ministry by reading from Isaiah 61, which is a description of the Messiah who will come, and saying "Today this Scripture has been fulfilled in your hearing." Translation: "Take a good look, gang. I'm the Messiah." That's a heckuva endorsement for us to think about. And that's not the only time he quotes Isaiah at a crowd.

Once Jesus makes that connection, it's easy to pick up on other similarities between Isaiah's messianic predictions and Jesus. The early Christians were all over it. So it's no surprise that Isaiah is quoted in the New Testament more than any other biblical book except Psalms. Let's dig in.

Quick Take on Isaiah

Isaiah wasn't interested in sharing his personal info. We do know he was married and had sons of his own. Mostly, Isaiah is all about getting God's message out there. In one of his most famous passages, Isaiah describes a vision in the temple that he is at the heavenly throne. Realizing his utter unworthiness, he cries out that he is a man of unclean lips. An angel fixes him right up by touching a burning coal to his lips. His guilt is removed! God then says, "Whom shall I send? Who will go for us?" Isaiah's fired up. "Here I am, send me!" And we're off and running for sixty more chapters of prophetic awesomeness.

Isaiah prophesied during the reigns of four kings of Judah,

so he may have been active for more than sixty years. He's got a great writing style, so good that he's been called the Shakespeare of prophets. If you love Hebrew poetry and imagery, you are in for a good time.

We all know the pain of washing whites and reds together.

His prophecies cover destruction in war, exile to Babylon, and rebuilding after the exile ends. There is a little history mixed in, so we can see the disaster of kings who trusted human alliances and the deliverance of kings who turned to God. The constant in these scenarios is God's tender love, reaching out continually to those who suffer. Yes, there is judgment; there is also salvation and mercy, peace and love.

Isaiah also prophesies a new creation, a new Jerusalem, and a new Davidic king (a.k.a. Messiah). These promises are why the Hebrew people hold Isaiah's book close to their hearts as the centuries go on with continued oppression from foreign powers. They are also what Jesus points to as predictions of his coming.

Living with Isaiah

Washing Those Sins Snowy White

First there's that burning coal. Not only does it purify Isaiah of his past sins, but it prepares him to speak for the Lord to others. You can only do that with a pure heart and mouth. But even before that, the Lord has a message for all of us.

> "Come now, let us reason together,
>   says the LORD:
> though your sins are like scarlet,
>   they shall be as white as snow;
> though they are red like crimson,
>   they shall become like wool." (Is 1:18)

We all know the pain of washing whites and reds together. You'll never get those whites really white again. This a great image that works across the ages. God can do this for us. In fact, he's pleading for us to take advantage of his offer, really selling the image so we understand just what he's offering.

All through Isaiah, we see God taking the initiative. And that's how it works in our lives, too. Isaiah's experience shows the pattern. God seeks out Isaiah, and just being in God's presence gives Isaiah a deep sense of self-knowledge. "Woe is me! For I am lost; for I am a man of unclean lips."

Remember Peter's early encounter with Jesus, which resulted in catching so many fish the boat was in danger of sinking? He had the same reaction. "Depart from me, for I am a sinful man, O Lord."

The right reaction to the presence of God is spiritual conversion, leading to a complete change of heart and life. And that time is now. Now is the moment when forgiveness is available, when we can realize our failures, our sins, our pride, and admit them to God.

God's forgiveness, his willingness and ability to get out those stains of sin, makes conversion and healing possible. Do I take advantage of that enough? When I forget who God really is and who I really am, the vast gulf between us as Creator and creature, I get into trouble, because sin doesn't seem like such a big deal anymore. I'm awfully glad to have the sacrament of confession, penance, reconciliation — call it what you want — to help get my head back in the right place.

When the Whole Country Is Going to the Dogs

Ah, the good old days. When everything was going great and folks just got along. News flash. Those days were … never.

There's nothing like reading history to remind us that each era has its own issues and problems to solve. That's Isaiah's story — through about two hundred years' worth of history. We encounter genuinely stupid leaders, genuinely powerless people, genuinely painful suffering and exile.

Isaiah shows us that a lot of the time we bring suffering

upon ourselves with our own bad decisions. Know-it-all kings get selfish and greedy. There goes the neighborhood to the foreign invaders again, because God's warnings are ignored and a purely human agenda can never foresee all the wrinkles.

Will anything ever change?

As it turns out, yes! Isaiah also shows us that things can change for the better if we turn to God, if we try to be a light to our own nation. God will not only heal our broken, suffering hearts, but he also will use us to reach out to others in need. Do I pray for my country? Do I respond in truth but also with love when there's an argument on social media? Do I defend the Church's teachings and make sure I'm educated in why I believe what she teaches? Am I living the Gospel in the world around me by helping out instead of ducking things that take me outside my comfort zone?

This is how we become the ones helping to bring our divided, frustrated, hurting nation out of exile and back into God's mercy and love.

The Fifth Gospel

Isaiah doesn't think of himself as predicting the future. He'll tell you he is simply proclaiming God's plan and revelation of himself. Past, present, future. What's the diff? It's all good, because it's all God. Not that this makes it easy for the kings he works with, who are all trying to turn Isaiah's prophecies to their own advantage — some for good, some for selfish reasons.

As I mentioned before, Jesus himself emphasizes how Isaiah's prophecies point to him as Messiah. The disciples need the clue. It isn't like these prophecies are easy to decipher. In a sense, they're hidden in plain sight. It sounds like a lovely dream to say, "Then the eyes of the blind shall be opened, and the ears of the deaf unstopped; then shall the lame man leap like a hart, and the tongue of the dumb sing for joy." Until you witness Jesus doing that very thing.

No wonder the apostles quote Isaiah so much in the New

Testament. They have seen the book come to life with their own eyes. In fact, from very early on, the Book of Isaiah was called "the fifth Gospel," because it includes so many predictions and descriptions of the future Messiah.

Some say that only gullible people believe predictions came true like that. They are forgetting that the Holy Spirit brings Scripture alive, speaks to us through it. The thing I love is that thinking about how the Book of Isaiah "spoke" to the apostles means we can expect the very same thing when we read the Bible. God has specific messages for us in plain sight, if only we take the time to read and pray using the Bible.

Chapter X

Jeremiah

He Cries Because He Cares

For I know the plans I have for you, says the L*ORD, plans for welfare and not for evil, to give you a future and a hope.*

Jeremiah 29:11

What to Read

The best place to get a good dose of the Book of Jeremiah is in the liturgy, where you can see what New Testament readings it's been matched up with for context.

Because Jeremiah isn't in chronological order, it can be hard to get a grip on for sampling. Here's a summary of how the book breaks down.

- Jeremiah 1: Call of Jeremiah
- Jeremiah 2–20: Judgment on Judah
- Jeremiah 21–35: Jeremiah's confessions and prophecies
- Jeremiah 36–45: Key historical events
- Jeremiah 46–51: Judgment on nations
- Jeremiah 52: Jerusalem's fall

Jeremiah needs encouragement, and so do the Hebrew people. His prophecies are loaded with warnings about fast-approach-ing, apocalyptic-scale tragedy, as well as some specific judgment against the way the people live. They need every bit of sunshine they can get.

Jeremiah is the longest book in the Bible. And it isn't in chronological order. Good times.

I'd like to say that there's nothing relevant for us in a book of international power shifts threatening annihilation; arrogant people who can't recognize their flaws (or sins) when one hits them in the face; and a guy who keeps trying to save his people no matter how many times they knock him down. Luke Skywalker. Black Panther. Captain Kirk. We all recognize this story; but when we tell it, the hero saves the day. No such luck here. This is a documentary, not fiction.

We know more about Jeremiah's internal life and feelings than that of any other prophet.

Jeremiah is a kind, courageous optimist. So it's kind of funny to find out he's nicknamed the "weeping prophet." It's because he's the only one who sees what's coming, and his people's refusal to listen to God's warnings is breaking his heart. There are tears. Lots and lots of tears.

We get the story in one of the biggest genre combinations in the Bible — sermons, confessions, lamentations, letters, history, dialogues with God, and more. One thing's for sure: You won't get bored.

Quick Take on Jeremiah

We know more about Jeremiah's internal life and feelings than that of any other prophet. This guy lets it all hang out. I can't blame him. Called to be a prophet when he's around seventeen, he famously protests that he's too young. God is having none of it, replying that he's created Jeremiah to be his prophet, and he'll protect him. Jeremiah recruits a secretary, Baruch, to record his prophecies. And we're off and running.

Jeremiah lives in a time during God's final warnings to the

people of Judah about their disbelief and disobedience. Those warnings have been coming for about nine hundred years, ever since his covenant with them in the desert. You can't say God isn't giving them a good, long grace period. Now it's judgment time. Jeremiah's job is to give the rulers one last chance to turn away from their sins. One good king and four bad ones later, the Babylonians show up. We've been hearing about this threat for a while. Hello Babylonian Exile, goodbye temple and Jerusalem. This experience will define the Hebrew people like nothing since the Exodus.

Jeremiah continually gives God's messages to the leaders and the people. In return he's mocked, accused of treason, beaten, abandoned in a muddy well, thrown in jail without parole and more. And for what? He's been getting nowhere for decades. Only a robot wouldn't get emotional at that point. Jeremiah is no robot, and he doesn't mind sharing.

As a result, Jeremiah does some of the most heartfelt, toughest questioning of God ever documented. No matter how frustrated he is, though, Jeremiah never forgets that God is like a fire burning in his bones. He always arrives at renewed commitment to God and a more loving relationship with him. Jeremiah builds on his divine friendship to point toward the coming Messiah, and the new covenant that will be inscribed in the heart of each believer. Thanks to all that sharing, the Hebrew people are able to use Jeremiah's experience of a personal relationship with God to keep their identity during seventy years of exile, and it transforms their religion by including the personal instead of just depending on the priesthood.

Living with Jeremiah

I Wish I Were Dead

If there's anything we know about Jeremiah, it's that he never holds back. So we know he's fighting mad when he tells God, "You seduced me, Lord, and I let myself be seduced" or "Cursed be the day on which I was born!"

This isn't the only time we see one of our prophets angry or depressed over his or her mission. In fact, this isn't the first time Jeremiah's complained to God, and it won't be the last. Jeremiah is famous for his laments. Check the next book in the Bible. Yep, Lamentations by our pal Jeremiah. However, this is the most all-encompassing moment I can think of. Jeremiah's not just ready to throw in the towel; he's throwing his very existence in God's face.

We've all had those "Why me, O Lord" moments. Fury and complaints are nothing new to God. But do we turn toward God or away from him in those moments? Every encounter with God, even an angry one, is a chance to discover something new about him or ourselves. We have to keep our eyes on God at that moment of rage to see what he wants of us now.

I've only been angry with God once in my life, but it was a deep, genuine rage. Years ago, I was with a group of Catholic women who brought up Saint Paul's direction to give thanks in all circumstances, because everything that happens is God's will. I had only listened, but turned it over in my mind on the way home. I suddenly thought of my daughter's deep depression, which had caused a lot of suffering. I was instantly enraged. Thank God? For my child's suffering? "How *dare* he expect me to give thanks! How dare he!"

It didn't last long. In fact, it might be the shortest rage with God on record. By the time I'd turned a corner and driven down the block to our house, I'd moved on to sullen acceptance. I went into my daughter's bedroom and told her we needed to give thanks for her illness. She was a lot more graceful about it than I was. We held hands and silently said our prayers. She looked at me and said, "I just realized that I was able to give a classmate advice about telling his mom he was depressed. I'd never have known to do it if I hadn't gone through this." In my turn, I had realized that her experience had given me insight and empathy when several friends had confided their own struggles with depression.

It's OK to be mad at God. Just remember that the point of expressing our anger is to honestly express deep feelings. We're not gonna tell God anything he doesn't already know, but if we're open to hearing his voice, then he'll be there helping us figure out stuff we didn't know. After all, he flat out tells Jeremiah: "You will seek me and find me; when you seek me with all your heart." That's the way forward out of anger.

God's Word Is Personal

Look up popular Jeremiah verses, and this comes out near the top:

> Now the word of the Lord came to me saying,
> "Before I formed you in the womb I knew you,
> and before you were born I consecrated you;
> I appointed you a prophet to the nations." (Jer 1:4)

We thrill to reflect on the fact that God formed us to be just the way we are. It has to be reassuring to Jeremiah to know that God created him to do this seemingly impossible job.

This quote, though, is the perfect window through which we can get a closer look at just how mad Jeremiah makes people. These verses form part of Catholic teachings on an issue that polarizes our society today in a way that nothing has since slavery: abortion.

Tertullian, reflecting on these verses in the first century, said: "The embryo therefore becomes a human being in the womb from the moment that its form is completed."

The Church never looks back from that basic truth. I was stunned to find the *Catechism* citing these verses as a biblical foundation for respecting and protecting human life. You can't avoid the fact that God's words in Jeremiah point toward a moral conclusion against abortion, even though it is not explicitly stated.

Are you mad at Jeremiah yet? Whether or not you are infuriated right now depends on which side of the abortion issue you stand. We're not here to argue that issue. It's one I struggled with myself when I entered the Church. Whether you are furious or not, you know how divisive and touchy that topic is. Imagine the reactions if someone walked through the streets of your town, loudly shouting, "Thus says the Lord, thou shalt not kill infants in the womb." They might get screamed at. Stoned. Shot.

This is a common theme with the prophets. God's law is personal. If it isn't this topic, just keep dipping into the Bible and Church teachings. You're gonna find something that enrages you, or at the very least troubles and annoys you.

That's because God not only loves you and me to the core, but he also loves every single person, no matter how imperfect we are. His perfect laws are there to bring every one of us to true happiness, not just people in your circumstances or mine. We can't always see that, though. That's exactly why we get so riled up when we're faced with the truth about something we hold a disagreeing opinion on.

The question at that point becomes, what will we do about it? Do we bury that infuriating truth and ignore it? Do we let it drive us away from God? Or do we acknowledge that it challenges and enrages — and then ask God for his help to understand and to change our ways to become his ways?

Baruch — The Ying to Jeremiah's Yang

Jeremiah needs a good friend because he gets the heck persecuted out of him. Hey, when you proclaim the truth and don't let people spin it into something they like better, you're gonna get the book thrown at you. In his day, the book includes getting dumped in a well, and prison without parole.

Baruch is called in because Jeremiah needs someone to set things down in writing. I like to think of them as two guys in a buddy road film, pulling pranks together during breaks in prophesying. Did they even like each other when they first met? No idea, but could they have stuck together all that time if there wasn't true friendship between them? If they didn't get along at the beginning, they sure do by the end.

Baruch is more than just Jeremiah's secretary. Jeremiah follows his advice. When Jeremiah's hiding to avoid a king's goon squad, Baruch steps in and reads his warnings to the people in the temple. They wind up under the same death threats together. They're in Jerusalem together during the Babylonian siege. When Jeremiah is taken to Egypt, Baruch goes, too.

We can't predict sometimes who will become our friends. Humphrey Carpenter in *The Inklings: C.S. Lewis, J.R.R. Tolkien, Charles Williams, and Their Friends* gives a classic example. C.S. Lewis was good friends with J.R.R. Tolkien, author of *The Lord of the Rings*. In fact, Lewis encouraged Tolkien to keep writing the book that would become so influential to generations of fantasy readers. Tolkien would get discouraged, and Lewis would say he wanted to read more. They did this for about fifteen years. The kicker is that when they met, they couldn't stand each other at first. It took them both joining the same club (to practice translating Norse mythology, the way you do) to get past bad first impressions and become good friends. That's the way it works when God is involved. He knows who we need as the perfect complement way before we figure it out.

It took me a long time to realize that friendship is a form of love that is a gift from God. Friendship is so unique and so necessary that it has been written about since ancient times as one of the highest virtues. Look at your friends and thank God for sending you the people that make life so rich. Especially for the ones you couldn't stand when you met them. He knows what he's doing.

Chapter XI

Ezekiel

Psychedelic Waters of Babylon

They had the form of men, but each had four faces, and each of them had four wings. Their legs were straight, and the soles of their feet were like the sole of a calf's foot; and they sparkled like burnished bronze. … As for the likeness of their faces, each had the face of a man in front; the four had the face of a lion on the right side, the four had the face of an ox on the left side, and the four had the face of an eagle at the back. … I saw a wheel upon the earth beside the living creatures, one for each of the four of them. … Their rims were full of eyes round about.

Ezekiel 1:5–18

What to Read

Just as with Isaiah and Jeremiah, the easiest place to read Ezekiel is in the liturgy of the Church. Reading how the prophecies are paired with Gospel readings often will shed light in both directions. Ezekiel is in chronological order, which is handy, but it can still be a beat-down with all the doom and gloom.

- Chapters 1–8 give you a good sample, and they aren't too long.
- Chapter 16 is the allegory of Jerusalem as an adulterous bride.

- Chapter 37 has the valley of bones and promises for the future kingdom.

OK, I'm officially freaked out. And that's just the angels. Ezekiel isn't even describing God yet. There is plenty more weirdness to come. No wonder angelic encounters usually begin with, "Do not be afraid." Um, too late.

I love science fiction, and I've seen a lot of superhero movies, but this stuff is nuts. This vision is how God gives Ezekiel fair warning that his prophet days are beginning. I've gotta admire Ezekiel. He doesn't flinch, but just gets down to it. The book he writes is one of the first pieces of apocalyptic literature ever. It helps us learn to expect mind-bending imagery from the genre (see Revelation in the New Testament for more).

Ezekiel makes every other prophet look like a sissy. Skeletons coming alive, giant wheels in the sky, Israel graphically described as a prostitute, and violent destruction are all thrown into one big pot with some bizarre performance art to make sure we get the point. God's totally ticked off. It's judgment time.

Quick Take on Ezekiel

Ezekiel was thirty, a priest, and living with his wife in exile in Babylon when he has his first vision. I love how bonkers it is — the wheels with eyes might be my favorite part.

Ezekiel delivers prophecies against Judah and Jerusalem. Like a much-loved wife who turns to prostitution, Jerusalem's idolatrous, disgusting behavior has earned her public punishment. The other nations will also face destruction — no one's off the hook here.

We've heard this basic message before. Jeremiah is laying it on the folks in Jerusalem right now, overlapping with Ezekiel. You'd think the Hebrews would get the point, but here we are. Maybe that's why things get ratcheted up to the next level, with Ezekiel symbolically acting out God's judgment by silently lying on his left side for 390 days and his right for another forty, shaving his head, building a scale model of Jerusalem and acting out the siege, dressing like an exile (a.k.a. stripping naked), and not mourning his dead wife. Et cetera. The people are used to prophets acting things out, but this is extreme even for them.

It's not all depressing. God sets the people free from collective responsibility. He wants a personal relationship with each and every one of them. "Have I any pleasure in the death of the wicked, says the Lord God, and not rather that he should turn from his way and live? … For I have no pleasure in the death of any one, says the Lord God; so turn, and live." God will help the people's inner conversion by giving them a new heart and a new spirit.

Ezekiel shares another new thing: God is not only found in the temple. A vision of God's presence leaving the temple to go be with the Babylonian exiles opens a new page of revelation for the Hebrews. He has not abandoned his people, even in the middle of a pagan country.

Eventually, news comes that Jerusalem has fallen. God's message changes to one hundred percent comfort. He promises that the people will get their country back, and the temple will be rebuilt. (Specific directions and measurements included.) And he'll return to the temple! Huzzah!

Ezekiel now has his famous vision of the valley filled with dry bones that become clothed with flesh. They form a living army to show that the kingdom of David will be restored. He's not actually using the word "Messiah," but we're hearing about a new exodus, creation, kingdom, and temple because of a certain once and future Shepherd-King. Jesus, anyone? That's what the first Christians saw here.

Living with Ezekiel

Putting the "Awe" in Awesome

Read chapter one slowly, and imagine it as you go. Artists through the ages have tried to portray this description of God on his throne surrounded by angels, so you're in good company.

To us it might sound pretty steampunk, with the lightning, wheels, and polished metal. But that's processing the images in very modern terms. The Hebrews would have seen hidden layers of meaning and imagery linking back to earlier books of the Bible. Heck, when I read about the rainbow surrounding God, even I flash back to God's promise to Noah to never destroy the earth again with water.

What it shows is the difficulty of translating angelic appearances and God's glory into language and concepts. Ezekiel reminds us that God is majestic, overpowering, and honestly, beyond our comprehension.

We don't talk about God's glory much these days, and it's not because we're confused by the imagery. To try to help us have an intimate relationship with God, awe is dropped in favor of someone who's like our best buddy. The downside is that it's pretty easy to ignore my buddy when he's telling me something I don't like.

Ezekiel emphasizes that God does care and is close to us. That can be hard to believe. On one hand, he is wearing rainbows. On the other hand, I'm hearing about an awful lot of punishment. How do we deal with this?

We have an advantage that Ezekiel didn't. Jesus Christ brings these contradictions together. Fully human, he is as close as I could ever want. Fully divine, he is awe-inspiring in a way I want to be worthy of.

I guess the question comes down to how I balance proper respect and awe with the closeness that Christ came to bring us. This is a balancing act that I am still working on. Ezekiel helps me keep the glory of God in mind, and that context makes Jesus' life and sacrifice even more awesome.

The Importance of Body Language

We are animals. Animals with immortal souls, but animals nonetheless. That means our communication goes beyond words. A hug. A wink. Singing. Crying. Riding bikes with a friend. Picking a flower for mommy. Licking the frosting spatula from your birthday cake. These experiences of body language can carry meaning beyond the mere physical.

God, who made us, knows this too. Ezekiel's very presence physically tells us God will not abandon his people. The prophet is a sign of God's enduring faithfulness. The prophet's job is to persevere in the truth. Boy, oh boy, does Ezekiel persevere. We've seen how he lives the message with his whole body.

Ezekiel's very presence physically tells us God will not abandon his people.

Jesus did the same. He was born to point us to a greater reality. He healed the sick. He walked on water. He washed the disciples' feet at the Last Supper. He died on the cross. Everything he did physically spoke of a deeper truth. That's why Christianity is rooted in the physical world, beginning with the Eucharist. We celebrate the resurrection not of an ethereal spirit, but of a flesh-and-blood man who ate fish before getting down to conversation.

The Catholic Church keeps true to this idea of experiencing the faith with our entire bodies. We kneel to pray. We fast. We smell incense and hear bells. We genuflect in front of the altar. We dip our fingers in holy water and cross ourselves. We eat the Body and Blood, soul and divinity of Christ when we partake of the Eucharist.

These physical elements of our faith remind us of our connection to God in a special way. Living the faith with our entire being also is a wordless witness to people around us. That is really important in a post-Christian world where there can be a tendency to think there aren't many believers around anymore. It points them to a greater reality, just as Ezekiel did. That's something to reflect on the next time I'm a bit embarrassed about praying before a meal in a restaurant or leaving ashes on my forehead on Ash Wednesday when I leave the church.

God's Shock Treatment

What happens when you have an addicted person in your life, and you're trying to get them to change? You hold an intervention. Because you'll go to any lengths to help them — even though they see your efforts as cruel.

In Ezekiel, God's people are so mired in sin that they won't even obey the laws of the pagan Babylonian gods. That's hardcore. Shock treatment's the only way to make them see reality. Not a problem — Ezekiel's all over it.

All through this harsh-sounding book, God keeps offering a fresh start. He rejoices when a wicked man turns from evil. "A new heart I will give you, and a new spirit I will put within you; and I will take out of your flesh the heart of stone and give you a heart of flesh." He'll restore everything, beginning with our hearts, if we only accept. That's where all change has to begin: from inside.

Even the harshest-sounding prophets include messages of God's love and mercy. God, who is outside of time, knows our potential to be rebellious and fall into sin, and he made Adam and Eve with free will anyway. He thinks we're worth it, worth fighting for, the way he does with the Hebrews in Ezekiel. He'll do the same for us when we're stubborn and lost.

I get it. I had a heart like a stone. I didn't even know that I did, but it showed in a hard, cynical attitude. When I found God, became Christian, became Catholic, I had to work to change my hardened secular heart to align with Catholic teachings. More than once I felt complete shock along the way, when God dropped some unbending truth on me. But he knew what I needed. Slowly, surely, God put a new spirit in me and gave me a heart of flesh.

The question is, what do we do when we get the wake-up call? We've got to be willing to change. It might hurt, but it can't be any worse than the mess we've gotten ourselves into.

Chapter XII

Daniel

Hero in a Strange Land

Therefore Daniel went in to Arioch, whom the king [Nebuchadnezzar] had appointed to destroy the wise men of Babylon; he went and said thus to him, "Do not destroy the wise men of Babylon; bring me in before the king, and I will show the king the interpretation."

Daniel 2:24

What to Read

- Daniel 1–6
- Daniel 7:13–14
- Daniel 12:1–3
- Daniel 13–14

The Book of Daniel isn't like the other major prophetic books. It's exciting, packed with stories about the king's court in Babylon. Some are familiar: Daniel in the lions' den, the three young men in the fiery furnace, the handwriting on the wall. These are staple illustrations in children's Bibles.

But there's always more to be gleaned from these familiar stories. I love that when Daniel is thrown into the lions' den, another king, Darius, is so upset that he can't eat or sleep. He can't even enjoy any fine entertainment. Who adds that kind of detail unless it really happened? They're totally best friends. You truly feel his joy when Daniel is alive in the morning.

Mix those kinds of stories with Daniel's prophetic dream visions, and you've got a real page-turner.

Quick Take on Daniel

Teenager Daniel and his three buddies, Jewish exiles in Babylon, are chosen to serve in King Nebuchadnezzar's household. They start trouble right away by refusing to eat the king's food, but are vindicated when their own food (prepared according to the Mosaic dietary laws) keeps them healthier. This starts a pattern of God's faithful support that will last through different tests and several kings.

Nebuchadnezzar is a tough boss. He orders all the wise men killed for not being able to describe his dream, before they even try to interpret it. That's one way to make sure your wise men aren't faking. Daniel, the foreign wise guy, perfectly describes the dream and interprets it, too. All because the one true God answers his prayers. I know who I want on my side.

Knocked out by Daniel's revelations, Nebuchadnezzar promotes the whole gang to government administration. When he sets up a ninety-foot-tall idol, and the three friends refuse to worship it, they get tossed — you guessed it — straight into the fiery furnace. An angel protects them, because God is faithful. The amazed king raises their ranks again. (That is one tough promotional ladder.)

The king has another dream, and Daniel's interpretation is true again when the king is stricken by God with madness. To be fair, it happens when he's walking around praising himself for his greatness. C'mon, Nebuchadnezzar. You've met Daniel's God. What did you expect? Luckily, he has a brief moment of reason, praises the one true God, and is restored to sanity.

Then there's a royal feast during which they use the sacred vessels from the Jerusalem temple as dinnerware. When a disembodied hand writes a mysterious message on the wall, the king shouldn't need his mother to tell him to fetch Daniel for translation. It doesn't make him look like the sharpest knife in the drawer. Daniel has bad news. The king has been weighed, judged, and found wanting. He will die and lose his kingdom — that very night.

New King Darius promotes Daniel, but jealous courtiers set him up, passing a law forbidding prayer to God. We know Daniel's never obeying that law, so into the lions' den he goes. Darius is on tenterhooks until the next morning. All the plotters and their families get thrown to the hungry lions, and a new law decrees that everyone reverence Daniel's God. The good guys win — again!

The next six chapters describe Daniel's visions, which have a lot to do with God's supremacy and pagan nations' ultimate destruction. No surprises there. This is the apocalyptic literature section, filled with crazy visions, though still more understandable than a lot of Ezekiel. However, there are some things that apply to Jesus and Christianity in a beautifully accurate way.

Daniel includes the first solid statement in the Old Testament about the resurrection of the body. He lays out the timing for the Messiah's arrival. (Guess what? Jesus shows up right when Daniel said.)* Daniel throws around the "son of man" phrase a lot, which Jesus picked up to describe himself, giving it a whole new meaning along the way.

The book ends with three final stories. 1) Beautiful Susanna is accused of adultery. Daniel proves her innocence. 2) The idol of Bel is consuming food and drink, so it must be a real god. Or is it? Daniel proves that's not so. 3) A dragon is worshiped as

---

* See Brant Pitre, John Bergsma, *A Catholic Introduction to the Bible: The Old Testament* (San Francisco: Ignatius Press, 2018), 898-901. "In short, for both Jerome and Eusebius — two giants among ancient Christian writers — the 'seventy weeks of years' — that is, 490 years — between the 'going forth of the word to restore and rebuild Jerusalem' (Dan 9:25) and the coming of an 'anointed one' (Dan 9:26) refers to the 490 years that elapsed between the time of King Artaxerxes of Persia's decree to rebuild the temple in the fifth century B.C. (see Ezra 7:11-26) and the coming of Christ in the first century A.D."

a god, but Daniel kills it. And we're back to the lions' den one more time, where God saves Daniel, and the king admits that God is the one true God.

Living with Daniel

Faithful in a Hostile Culture

How does a faithful worshipper manage when surrounded by a godless culture? That's the big question for Daniel, and we find ourselves facing the same problems today.

What's interesting about Daniel's situation is that he's not dealing with deliberately evil people. They honestly don't know what is true. In fact, a lot of the time they come to Daniel for answers. So what does Daniel do? Not what you'd probably expect.

Daniel and his friends serve with loyal expertise and unfailing excellence. Daniel's patience and honesty lead to friendship and influence on royalty. Can you work with pagans and remain committed to God? Daniel shows us the answer is yes.

Where Daniel comes into conflict with the Babylonians is in his faith. Check out what "conflict" means to Daniel, though. When he's challenged, he doesn't lash out. He invites scientific investigation, such as going on a trial period of eating his own food instead of the king's food to see which is better. Clinical results? Daniel wins. If Daniel or his friends suffer punishment, they accept it and put all their faith in God and continual prayer.

A lot of us are in Daniel's shoes. We've lost a culture war, not an actual war.

A lot of us are in Daniel's shoes. We've lost a culture war, not an actual war. We're surrounded by secular pagans in a culture that doesn't care much about or actively despises Christianity. But by being visible Christians, we keep our world from being a much worse place. Daniel's adventures are like a template for how to change the culture from the inside: honest service, faithful friendship, calm defense of your faith, coupled with prayer and relationship with God.

When you meet someone who is strikingly honest, loyal, friendly, and faithful, don't you want to know how they're so great? This is what Daniel did. This is what the first-century Christians did in Rome. This is what we can do too, right here in our own time.

Fighting Temptation

Jesus was tempted in the wilderness and the temple, and on the mountaintop — a place of testing, a place of worship, and a place of personal encounter with God. So, just in case we thought we'd ever be free from temptation, that's a hard no.

What to do? Temptations follow wherever we go. I admit that a lot of the time I don't want to resist. My temptations are tailor-made, after all, to strike just where I'm weakest. I already know it's easy to give in "just once." And then my inclinations grow stronger, and I give in "just once" again. Eventually I'm not fighting a temptation any more. I've developed a habit. And now I have an even bigger problem.

Daniel and his friends are good examples of how to resist temptation. You've got to know what you believe in and where to draw the line. Daniel knew what his faith required, and he was committed to it, so he was prepared to resist. He didn't argue or waffle or consider the wrong options. He sought to please God above all.

When you look at Jesus' temptations and life, the same pattern, divinely perfected, comes through: prayer, trust in God, regular practice in resisting temptation (such as fasting). Paul tells us, "Put on the whole armor of God, that you may be able to stand against the wiles of the devil." And even he complains that "a thorn was given me in the flesh, a messenger of Satan" sent to bother him.

Will these strategies work every single time? No, because we're human. But every time we fight off temptation, we're a little stronger. It's gonna make us stronger for the fight and prone to fall less.

Hard-Boiled Detective

In a lot of ways, Daniel makes me think of a noir-style detective. He doesn't have a fedora, a bottle of bourbon in his desk drawer, or cigarettes, but his innate sense of honor and dedication to truth just won't quit. Isn't that what you expect from a detective? And a man of God? Funny how those two things coincide.

Two stories about Daniel are the earliest detective stories ever. In Susanna and the Elders, we hear two lecherous elders' "foolproof" plan to get Susanna to sleep with them. She rejects them, and — oh no! — Susanna's immediately sentenced to death. Daniel's skilled questioning proves the two accusers never bothered to get their stories straight.

"Taking his stand in the midst of them, [Daniel] said, 'Are you such fools, you sons of Israel? Have you condemned a daughter of Israel without examination and without learning the facts? Return to the place of judgment. For these men have borne false witness against her.' … And Daniel said to them, 'Separate them far from each other, and I will examine them.'"

Case closed. Susanna is set free.

The story of Bel is a classic locked-room mystery. Every night the idol of the pagan god Bel eats sacrifices left in a locked, sealed room. Daniel doesn't know what's going on, but he does know that no clay idol can eat forty sheep a night. Daniel spreads ashes on the floor after the night's sacrifice is set up. In the morning, footprints in the ash force the corrupt priests to admit they've been stealing the offerings through a secret door.

Mysteries fit right into a book about a prophet, because they make us long for justice and truth and redemption. The truth always comes out no matter how much chaos there is, how few things make sense, or how much suspicion is sowed. There is always a right answer. That's what we all long for, not just in detective stories but in life.

Daniel reminds us that there is such a thing as truth. He's stubborn and doesn't give a damn about popular opinion. He won't take the easy way out. That's what makes him so successful; not just in these mysteries, but every time he's asked to do something that strikes his conscience as wrong.

I don't have to deal with any real-life mysteries except for "where did I leave my phone?" But there are lots of practical mysteries that pop up in living my faith. "Why does the Church have this teaching? How do I explain it to my kid, a stranger, a mean atheist?" True story. I've been stuck more than once publicly explaining some of the most embarrassing teachings of our time, at least embarrassing as far as our modern culture is concerned.

The only solution is Daniel's. Investigate. Question. Test. Know your faith. And pray like crazy while trusting in God. There is truth and a right answer. We've just got to be hard-boiled and stubborn. Fedoras optional.

Chapter XIII

Hosea

Not Family Friendly

And I will espouse you to me for ever; I will espouse you to me in righteousness and in justice, in steadfast love, and in mercy. I will espouse you to me in faithfulness; and you shall know the LORD.

Hosea 2:19–20

What to Read

- Chapters 1–4, 11, 14

Israel's got an idol problem. Its people keep leaving their loving one true God for flings with a pagan god.

Hosea's got a marriage problem. The love of his life, Gomer, is unfaithful and keeps playing around with other men, sometimes for money.

This is a not-safe-for-work book of the Bible. Prostitution, adultery, sexual imagery, shaming, and diehard vengeance make this one for adults only. But you'll also find hope, compassion, reconciliation, and steadfast love in these pages. And those *are* things you can share around work and with the whole family.

We've all heard God loves us, but did you ever wonder how much? Spread your arms out as far as they'll go. That's right — thiiiiiiiiiiis much and more. So much that he got Hosea to make his entire life into our example. It's tough on Hosea, but that's a prophet's life most of the time.

Quick Take on Hosea

Hosea is a sensitive, tenderhearted guy who is married to a prostitute. He married her on God's direct orders; but, to be fair, he seems to genuinely love her. We don't know whether she was a prostitute when they got married or turned to it later. Some people think she was a cult prostitute serving the pagan god Baal. What we do know is that she was repeatedly unfaithful, to the point where Hosea was not the father of some of their children. That hurts. We feel for him bitterly.

Gomer's continual betrayal leaves Hosea jealous, angry, and brokenhearted. In spite of everything, he still passionately loves her. So much so that he reconciles with her even after she's left him for another man. And that's something that was unthinkable at the time. Do his buddies give him a hard time over this? I can hear the jokes now. That doesn't stop Hosea. He's willing to be vulnerable and honest. He paints a picture of his life with emotional power and gorgeous poetry.

That's just the first three chapters. The rest of the book is Hosea using his own life as an example to try to make Israel understand that their covenant with God is as personal and intimate as a marriage. When they worship pagan gods, it's not just "breaking the rules." It's deeply personal betrayal.

There is punishment, but the point is to bring the people back to God. It's like a doctor operating, or a dentist filling a cavity. Sometimes painful treatment is necessary to allow healing to begin. God's steadfast love never wavers, and he is always ready to offer forgiveness and self-giving love.

God is shown being wounded, jealous, grieving, loving, and romantic, all human characteristics. Keep in mind that this isn't literally the case — God isn't really experiencing these human emotions — but we can't understand the mystery of God, so Hosea's very human language gives us a glimpse into how the people's infidelity affects their relationship with God.

Living with Hosea

When God Asks You to Do Something Really Hard — And You're Not Getting Any Benefits

"The LORD said to Hosea: 'Go, get for yourself a woman of prostitution and children of prostitution, for the land prostitutes itself, turning away from the Lord."

Wait, what? This seems like the worst treatment of any prophet ever. You'd like to think that "a match made in heaven" would result in your soul mate, not someone who's going to break your heart over and over. When God himself arranges your marriage and then promises that your wife's going to commit adultery, that just doesn't seem right.

How does Hosea feel about this? Actions speak louder than words. No dillydallying. He follows God's orders instantly. A world of heartbreak is soon his. We hear about his feelings when he's suffering from betrayal and faithlessness, but that doesn't stop his obedience.

God can ask unbelievable obedience of prophets living in difficult times. Often they get no reward. We're not ancient Hebrew prophets, but the times we live in might be just as difficult as Hosea's. What if God asks me to do something unbelievably weird or hard? How would I respond? I've faced small challenges that seemed really difficult, but there was almost always an immediate reward when I conquered my reluctance. How about the times when there isn't an obvious benefit for me, but only for others?

This is something Jesus talks about: "If any man would come after me, let him deny himself and take up his cross and follow me." That's the example Hosea sets, and it's what we see from the saints. I'm no prophet, and I'm not a saint yet. But what if one day God gave me a difficult mission? Could I jump to obey, trusting in God's plan and his love? Pondering that question might just be the thing that gets me ready for the next personal challenge I face.

When Ordinary Life Opens the Way for God

Hosea's personal life flows into his teachings. It helps connect the people to God's message. They understand love, betrayal, and longing. His example is right in front of them. That lets Hosea push it up to the next level, where they can understand how their own actions betray God's love.

You don't have to be a prophet for your personal life to point to God. We're busy, and he knows it. So, just as with Hosea, he meets us in ordinary circumstances, opportunities, and people to get our attention. A crazy car accident, that lucky job opportunity, your best friend's good advice — any one of those can point to his vision of how your life should be.

You don't have to be a prophet for your personal life to point to God.

That's how God invites our complete cooperation. We fully live our Christian lives by doing our everyday best throughout the good, the bad, and the ugly. I get this thing right, I get that thing wrong. Looking at my personal history through his gaze, I understand more deeply how my actions and relationships lead me closer to or further away from him. And the people around us pay attention to how we respond to God. Our examples might just help some of them move a little closer to God, too.

Never Give Up, Never Surrender

Hosea can be a tough book to recommend. A quick look around the internet finds women bashing it for spousal abuse, pornography, female oppression, and more. (Look, it's prophecy, not a marriage manual.)

So I was surprised to meet a young woman who says this is her favorite book of the Bible. A former atheist, she delights in the descriptions of God's unceasing forgiveness and tender love, especially for those who won't give him the time of day.

That makes sense to me. Who doesn't want to find a fresh, pure love that is unlike any other, completely satisfying yet ever new?

Hosea continually describes Israel as ignorant of God. Israel doesn't understand God and so has no desire to please him. No wonder, like Gomer, its people chase after other loves. They worship false gods. So old-fashioned, right? Except that we modern people also look for happiness and fulfillment in a lot of places that have nothing to do with God. Our society is obsessed with wealth, beauty, pleasure, and influence. Those false idols lead to chaos and heartbreak instead of a secure foundation. It happens all the time.

God knows and loves each of us for who we are, and so he knows what we need better than we do. And he never gives up. His love is always there. That's what that young woman discovered. It's what I discovered when I opened my agnostic heart to ask God if he existed. And each of us has the chance to discover this love for ourselves. Have other loves replaced God in our hearts? Do we chase other idols because we don't know God? It's never too late to turn to him.

He's waiting. Because he never gives up.

Chapter XIV

Amos

Sticking It to the Man

But let justice roll on like a river, righteousness like a never-failing stream!

Amos 5:24, NIV

What to Read

- All nine super-short chapters

Amos wouldn't join one of those wimpy prophets' guilds if they paid him. He's a farmer and a shepherd with no use for uppity rich folk. He calls the women "cows of Bashan" and tells a priest that his wife will be a prostitute.

Amos has the word of the Lord, and he's not soft-pedalling it. Just the truth: plain, simple … and extremely blunt. Hey, he's a farmer, not a prophet. Take it or leave it.

Amos is oldest of the prophetic books (the books that solely report prophecies and occasional deeds). No history involved. Amos wasn't the first prophet by a long shot, but the themes he covers will be touched on by every prophet who follows him. Buckle up.

Quick Take on Amos

Amos is hardcore. Poetic, but hardcore. His is the fire-and-brimstone preaching that the Old Testament has a reputation for being loaded with. The Israelites are all show when it comes to religion, with no true love of God in their hearts. Their arrogance, materialism, and injustice will lead to them being carried off into exile.

What's interesting is that Amos doesn't treat Israel any differently than any of the other nations. He's an equal opportunity prophet. First, he condemns all nations (they each get a turn), because they should all be following the universal laws of justice that are obvious to everyone. Then he gets to Israel. They aren't exempt because of their relationship with God. In fact, they've gotten special instructions and extra help. So why aren't they a better example to everyone else? Hmmm?

Five visions signal divine judgment and imminent destruction. God's unloading the whole package on them, because that's what hypocrisy and oppression of the poor earns you.

Finally, Amos gets to God's love and mercy — in the last five verses. He's not handing out sunshine and lollipops here. Leave that to the prophets who follow him. There's reform to be done. Best to get on with it.

Living with Amos

Face to Face with the Poor

The first time I ever saw a beggar was in Paris, many years ago. She was across the street, and my husband said, "Don't look at her." Completely fascinated, I looked over … and turned away quickly when she began screaming and shaking her fist at me. It's probably a good thing I wasn't very fluent in French. There were beggars everywhere. It was deeply troubling for someone like me, who had never seen such a thing before. My husband had lived in London and was more blasé. He taught me to ignore them, and that beggars made good money. I did make him give to a couple of war veterans playing music. After all, they had sacrificed and deserved our charity.

But what about the people who don't "deserve" it, the ones

who are just poor? What about the homeless person who walks up to your car window when you're stopped at a light? What if it's a scam? Let's face it. I'm not smart enough to figure it out, especially before the light changes. Because what if they are in dire need, and I am the one God sent to them for help? Saint John Vianney gives it to us straight. We've got no excuses after reading his comments:

> There are those who say to the poor that they seem to look to be in such good health: "You are so lazy! You could work. You are young. You have strong arms."
>
> You don't know that it is God's pleasure for this poor person to go to you and ask for a handout. You show yourself as speaking against the will of God.
>
> There are some who say: "Oh, how badly he uses it!" May he do whatever he wants with it! The poor will be judged on the use they have made of their alms, and you will be judged on the very alms that you could have given but haven't.

Things weren't that different back in Amos's day. There were plenty of scams, incredible wealth, and crushing poverty. Amos knows God will sort it out. After all, the Lord judges those who give and those who receive. What would Amos say today? That my job is to give to the poor. What will of God's am I thwarting because I'm afraid of a scam? Who's left hungry because I'm trying to be savvy?

Vacation Every Week — I Insist

One of my favorite bits of Amos is when he scolds the merchants for outwardly observing the sabbath while simultaneously plotting how to cheat the poor in the marketplace tomorrow.

I know I'm not the only one who drifts into a mental to-do list during Mass. To be fair, I'm thinking a lot less about "cheating the poor" and more about rearranging my Monday schedule so I can make it to my book club. But I'm not focusing on God; I'm actually working.

I can't think of any commandment that we ignore as regularly as the third one: "Remember the sabbath day, to keep it holy. Six days you shall labor, and do all your work; but the seventh day is a sabbath to the Lord your God; in it you shall not do any work." This commandment is so important that it comes before the ones about honoring your parents and not committing murder. And it's not a request. It's a command. One that we are often tempted to ignore.

Maybe we ignore the command because we think of it as being for God's good instead of our own. But God needs nothing, especially not time off. We're the ones who need a vacation. God just wants us to take one every week to keep holy by not working. In other words, by resting. Of course, one way we keep it holy is by attending Mass. There's no better way to honor God than by this worship. But other than that? Every time it is mentioned, the only commandment on how to keep the day holy is by not working (Ex 20:8; 34:21; Dt 5:12–15).

What's interesting is that God doesn't dictate how, exactly, we choose to take rest — only that we do so. The rest itself is the thing that's holy. Talk about freedom!

I'm not saying it's easy, especially at first. When you're in the habit of using Sunday for crossing things off your to-do list, it's hard to stop. It means rearranging your schedule. It means Saturdays become super busy. You realize just how addictive it is to "get things done." But guess what? The list will still be there after a break, and you will find yourself better able to check things off of it. So take a little day off, per the Lord's instructions.

Suddenly you'll find time on Sunday to take a walk, ride bikes, write in your journal, call your mom, play a game with the kids, learn the guitar, or take a nap — all those things that never make it onto the list in the first place.

This wasn't easy for our family. Not easy at all. Even now we still backslide into fitting in a bit of work here and there. But when we stick to our guns, our Sundays are heavenly. And that's really the point. Those leisurely Sundays are what life is supposed to be like all the time. Just a little taste of heaven on Earth. We are supposed to be working for the Sabbath, for the day that refreshes, that makes life fully worth living.

Begin with an hour or two each Sunday, and don't stop. Gradually build up to a whole day of "holy rest." Trust your manufacturer. He knows what you need.

Coming Alive for the Master

What's a farmer doing so far from home, giving people the what-for? I know God has given him a message to deliver. But I wonder whether Amos already has such a sympathy for the poor and a love for God that he's especially open to God's call.

I wonder whether Amos already has such a sympathy for the poor and a love for God that he's especially open to God's call.

God's gifts to us are supposed to benefit everybody. We don't think of it that way. We just think we're lucky in some of our qualities. We naturally use them in our lives. But how do we use them to serve God?

A friend once told me that I have the charism of hospitality. A charism is a spiritual gift (as of healing) given by the Holy Spirit for the good of the Church. Charisms give us an effectiveness that transcends our natural, human abilities.

Hospitality as a charism? Maybe. What I do know is that hearing that talent called out so specifically makes me think about the ways I am hospitable. It encompasses my love of cooking, desire to make everyone comfortable, joy in seeing a group have a great time together, ability to set people at ease, and even organizational skills. When the kids were teenagers, ours was the home where their friends came for big get-togethers. We're lucky to have a house with a big living room, so we often host our parish's marriage retreat team meetings, my Catholic women's book club, and more. I love all these people we host, and if hospitality is how we show it, then all the better.

What about your own charisms and talents? Maybe you're good with kids, so you could help with religious education. If you're good at explaining things logically, have you thought about using that talent to explain or defend the faith? Do you love to cook? What about volunteering to help with meals for the homeless? Taking our eyes off ourselves and offering our skills to Jesus opens our lives to be formed to his will and our joy.

Will you be embarrassed sometimes? Challenged? Have to take risks? Maybe. But responding to that inner call gives true freedom. It is thrilling and fulfilling unlike anything else.

Chapter XV

Jonah

Mad as Hell and Running from God

But Jonah rose to flee to Tarshish from the presence of the LORD. He went down to Joppa and found a ship going to Tarshish; so he paid the fare, and went on board, to go with them to Tarshish, away from the presence of the LORD.

Jonah 1:3

What to Read

- All four short, exciting chapters.

I've got to hand it to Jonah; he doesn't mess around. God gives him a prophecy to deliver, and in the second sentence, Jonah's on the run, "fleeing." Look at how the next verse almost trips over itself to get all the information out. No question about it. Jonah's getting away from God as far and fast as he can.

The Book of Jonah is not only short, it is a story. That's a huge win when it comes to the prophets, who usually just give us their long, long speeches. Jonah is suspenseful, exciting, and funny. It also invites us to examine our own response to God when we're asked to do something we don't like. That's a lot for four short chapters, but Jonah delivers.

You might think you know the story. Who doesn't hear "Jonah" and think "swallowed by a whale?"

But Jonah's packed with details I never noticed until I sat down and read it with full attention. Every one of them matters. The last time I read it I fell in love with the sailors, because they try rowing to shore instead of automatically tossing Jonah overboard, even when they know he's the reason for the storm. I never even noticed those sailors before. It's always worth reading Scripture more than once, because you don't know what you'll find that makes the story come alive.

Quick Take on Jonah

God tells Jonah to preach in Nineveh. Nineveh's the capital of Assyria, the most powerful and ruthless nation of the time, which all Israelites reading this book would've known. Not a place you just want to pop into. Jonah, as we have seen already, hot-foots it in the opposite direction to a ship at the edge of the known world. God raises a huge storm, causing the pagan sailors to toss Jonah overboard, where God saves him by having a huge fish swallow him. Bonus: The sailors begin worshipping God.

After three days and three nights, the fish vomits Jonah onto dry land. (Vomits. You've got to love the way the Hebrews keep it real. Jonah gets zero respect.) God repeats his command and, unsurprisingly, Jonah finally obeys.

And — are you ready for this? — the people of Nineveh surprise everyone, probably including themselves, by believing Jonah the very first day and promptly doing penance. They also make their animals do penance. These Ninevites are all in. This might be a first in the history of biblical prophecy.

God forgives them, which makes Jonah hopping mad. He furiously sits on a hill, watching the city, wishing he were dead, and complaining to God that this is why he ran away. "I knew you would forgive them," he says. God has a plant grow, providing Jonah with much-needed shade, and then has a worm attack the plant so it withers and dies. Jonah gets even more infuriated, giving God some great talking points. The ensuing conversations provide God's point of view.

Living with Jonah

Mad as Hell

Let's face it: Jonah himself is not a great person. He hates the Ninevites so much. It's hard to blame him, because the Ninevites are the worst, a lot like ISIS and the Nazis rolled into one. So he runs.

Jonah isn't simply being disobedient. He knows Scripture well enough to deeply disagree with God's probable attitude to the Ninevites. In Exodus, God gives Moses the tablets and describes his nature: "The LORD, the LORD, a God merciful and gracious, slow to anger, and abounding in steadfast love and faithfulness, keeping steadfast love for thousands, forgiving iniquity and transgression and sin, but who will by no means clear the guilty."

It's the only place in the Old Testament where God describes his own nature,* and you can bet Jonah knew it. Did Jonah want that for the Ninevites? Heck no!

It's ironic that Jonah's absolute faith in God's true nature is horribly justified when God forgives them at the first opportunity. Jonah comes right out and says, "Is not this what I said when I was yet in my country? That is why I made haste to flee to Tarshish; for I knew that thou art a gracious God and merciful, slow to anger, and abounding in steadfast love, and repentest of evil."

Mic drop.

What a powerful message this is for the Israelites reading this book. Their whole culture revolves around being God's chosen people, whether or not they actually obey him very well. Now this clever book preaches a subversive message of God's equal love for all peoples, all nations, and all creation.

Unfortunately, I understand Jonah all too well. I haven't had

---

* J. Carl Laney, "God's Self-Revelation in Exodus 34:6-8," *Bibliotheca Sacra* 158 (January-March 2001): 36-51, https://www.galaxie.com/article/bsac158-629-03

a lot of violence enter my life, but his feelings about the Ninevites match the thirst for vengeance I felt on 9/11. I hated the terrorists, and I equally hated the Middle Eastern women I saw on TV exulting in the death and destruction of my beloved countrymen. How dare they!

It seems to be human nature, doesn't it? We want justice. Mercy isn't even on our radar. The troubled look in a gentle friend's eyes when I told her my feelings finally made me stop and reconsider my lust for vengeance. I was able to let my hatred go when I leaned on the truth expressed by God at the end of Jonah: "And the LORD said … 'And should not I pity Nineveh, that great city, in which there are more than a hundred and twenty thousand persons who do not know their right hand from their left, and also much cattle?'" Those women didn't know any better, and I did. That made it my responsibility to take control of my feelings.

Which Hand Is Which?

Any time that someone tells you the "Old Testament God" is cruel and vengeful, remember the Book of Jonah. Absolutely not. God is God, no matter which Testament we're reading. The mercy he shows the Ninevites is the same mercy we see Jesus praying for from the cross, "Father, forgive them; for they know not what they do."

When I'm embarrassed over things I've done in the past, I remember God's understanding words about the Ninevites, which I think are some of the most loving and hopeful in the entire Bible.

When I'm embarrassed over things I've done in the past, I remember God's understanding words about the Ninevites.

God knows that the Ninevites are ignorant, that they never had an opportunity to learn another way, and that they haven't been given a real chance to be anyone other than who they are. And he knows that about me. As an agnostic, I made fun of people who remained chaste before marriage; called the Eucharist "that cracker"; and rolled my eyes over the pro-life movement. It has taken a lot of time, a lot of reading, and much internal prompting from God for me to be able to see things from his point of view. I appreciate now how ignorant I was and how obnoxious I must have seemed to Christians around me.

It's why I also appreciate his gentle correction as I try — sometimes enthusiastically, sometimes halfheartedly — to live my life as a faithful Catholic, in Jesus' footsteps.

Running from God

I'm like Jonah in more ways than one. I can be pretty quick off the mark in the wrong direction when God calls with something I don't want to do.

What's worse, a lot of the time I'm pretending to myself that I'm not turning my back on God. For all Jonah's faults, he never pretended he wasn't defying God. He even understood his own motivations. I'm not that honest a lot of the time.

My problems are all pretty small compared with having to go declare God's word to a hostile nation: the acquaintance that I don't want to invite to a party because she is awkward to be around. The evenings I don't want to give up to volunteer. The sick person I don't want to visit because he can be pretty critical.

These petty problems can loom large, and I know I sound exactly like a sulky teenager when I'm coming up with excuses. And, come to think of it, so does Jonah, when he's on the hill overlooking the city. Just as Jonah only cared that the plant was dying because he lost the shade, not for the plant's sake, we often think of everything (including people) according to how it affects us, not for another's sake. That is where God's thought-provoking question to Jonah comes in at the end.

We're not given an answer to God's question. Instead we, like Jonah, are left to ponder God's ways and our own. Do I want to be like Jonah? Or just go ahead and try it God's way? Because the only one I'm fooling is myself.

Chapter XVI

Habakkuk

The Solution Is Worse than the Problem

O LORD, how long shall I cry for help,
and you wilt not hear?
Or cry to thee "Violence!"
and you wilt not save?

Habakkuk 1:2

What to Read

- All three chapters of peppy dialogue

Habakkuk's the guy for when everything is terrible, and I mean everything — society, government, the Church, the world in general — and you cry out to God to fix things. Now! Of course, God's idea of an awesome solution might not be just what we had in mind. And that's when we really need Habakkuk.

Habakkuk is a minor prophet during a time when there are a slew of prophets around, including Jeremiah, Daniel, Ezekiel, Obadiah, and Nahum. You can't say God isn't trying to get the word out to his people. There are prophets everywhere pointing out God's perspective. In fact, one of my favorite bits of overlap is from the Book of Daniel. Habakkuk's just fixed a tasty stew for some field hands in Judah when an angel grabs him by the hair and flies him to a Babylonian lions' den for lunch delivery to Daniel. (Why not just grab the bowl?) But Habakkuk's tough. He can take it.

Habakkuk keeps it short and sweet, getting his job done in just three chapters. He goes toe-to-toe with God, pushing back when he doesn't like the answer, but remaining honest enough to embrace God's will no matter what. These three chapters are a dialogue with God that drops us right into the action and won't let us turn away until we've wrestled with why God doesn't instantly make the world a better place.

Quick Take on Habakkuk

We know less about Habakkuk than just about any other prophet. This guy's not in it to get to know us. He's riled up and challenging God for his inaction. Everything about Jewish society is sinful: They've got unjust judges, cheating politicians, oppression of the poor, idol worshipping, and violence. So why isn't God doing anything?

Unlike a lot of other times in the Bible, God speaks right up. There's an amazing plan in the works, he tells Habakkuk. No one's going to believe how great it is. God's going to use the Chaldeans (Babylonians) to end the corruption. Just to be sure Habakkuk's got the picture, God gives a really thorough description of what awesome, epic conquerors they are.

Wait. What?

Did God just say that the solution is to let the bad guys destroy them? OK, Habakkuk knows that if anyone is justified in harsh chastisement, it's God. But this seems extreme. There's no need to tell Habakkuk about the Chaldeans' mad war skills. Everyone has been watching them crush the Assyrians, who are no slouches as conquerors. The Chaldeans are bad news; and, for that matter, bad guys. If God is so holy that he can't tolerate evil, then how can these bad guys be part of his plan? They'll flourish while the innocent die? After all, not every Jew is corrupt. How can this be God's justice? This is just plain shocking and confusing.

Habakkuk doesn't keep these questions to himself, respectfully telling God that he's got some 'splainin' to do. Then he settles back. He's a man of faith. And he's fair. He's going to wait, listening carefully, for God to answer his question, and God won't fail him. He'll give God time.

The answer? "Wait." Everyone's favorite answer.

His faith is justified when God does reply. The answer? "Wait." Everyone's favorite answer. He tells Habakkuk to write this one down so everyone knows, because it might take a while, but this plan is bigger than just the one part he told Habakkuk. The difference between faithful and unfaithful does matter. "The just one who is righteous because of his faith shall live." This is a hint that a remnant of Israelites will live. The Chaldeans' turn will come. Ultimately, they will reap the destruction they've sown by their violence and idolatry, even if it will be too late for Habakkuk and his community.

Whew! At last things make sense, even if the Israelites are going to be really sorry, really soon. Habakkuk prays a psalm of praise for what God's done for his people in the past and what he promises for their nation's future. Even though he's shaking in his shoes about the bad times coming, he will trust God.

Living with Habakkuk

> I will take my stand to watch,
> and station myself on the tower,
> and look forth to see what he will say to me,
> and what I will answer concerning my complaint.
> (Hb 2:1)

I first encountered Habakkuk in these lines. I'd flipped open my Bible during my prayer time. These words met my eyes, and I liked them. I liked the idea of someone who would steadfastly keep waiting for God's answer. I liked the idea of a loyal soldier guarding the heart of the city against something that might break the walls down. And I discovered that something was coming to literally tear down those walls. In eight short years, the Chaldeans will conquer Habakkuk's beloved Jewish people.

But I didn't know that at the time. I looked at that passage and thought of all the times that I was forced to wait for God's answer, because there was no one else to whom I could go. I thought of the patience his plan had required to get me to where I could begin to believe in the God I was asking questions of.

I wondered what question Habakkuk was waiting for an answer to, so I read the first chapter and fell in love with Habakkuk. He doesn't pussyfoot around. He is honest, straightforward and passionate. He knows God well enough to be outraged by silence when there is great need. He challenges God's plan of imminent destruction for his people.

So what does he do? He sits and waits, with an open mind.

And he listens.

I can't count the number of times Habakkuk's watching and waiting have stood as a great example when I've needed to trust God. How often have I told God the way things need to be done? How often have I wailed and moaned and filled all the space with my own voice? We all know the answer: too often.

Habakkuk reminds me that sometimes the only responses we can have toward God are silence, waiting, and listening. And trusting.

Things Are Getting Messy

There's a certain comfort in reading God's words here:

> For still the vision awaits its time;
>   it hastens to the end — it will not lie.
> If it seem slow, wait for it;
>   it will surely come, it will not delay. (Hb 2:3)

The plan will all work out, but it's going to take time to get everything set up. Everything will happen when it should.

That's fine when it's just a story. When a prophet from ancient days sees no way out, I think "Poor Habakkuk," and I shut my Bible and check email. But when my life works the same way, it's not fun at all. There are times when I'm in it neck-deep, and the tide is coming in. I'm lost, I'm struggling, I'm confused, I'm on the fence. The stakes are high, and there's no way out. I want relief, I want answers, and I want them now. But God is silent.

Sometimes life isn't about what we're supposed to do. Sometimes, as we see in Habakkuk, it's about what we need to endure while we wait for God to work. The problem is not with God, but with our limited understanding. We have to remember God's promise in these moments. He is there, plans are under way, and everything is ordered for our ultimate good, whether we know it or not. We're not in control, and that's OK.

Whom Can You Trust?

In the end, everything boils down to Habakkuk's relationship with God. The Chaldean freight train is going to run his people down. God has promised, so it's happening. How Habakkuk gets through the suffering — and possibly is able to help his people — depends on his attitude toward God. He actually has a full-on anxiety attack at the thought of the future. He says: "I hear, and my body trembles, my lips quiver at the sound; rottenness enters into my bones, my steps totter beneath me." But having meditated on who God really is in his psalm of praise, Habakkuk trusts God's promise, even if he will be left with no food or possessions.

This whole questioning process seems to have begun an internal change in Habakkuk. Perhaps he has grown closer to God? He began by complaining about God's silence and lack of action. He ends up rejoicing and exulting in his saving God. God's gifts and protection are easy to praise, but Habakkuk rejoices despite God's promise of suffering and no security. This is the faith of someone who has spoken with God, heard his answers, and who has a real relationship with God.

It seems to me that Habakkuk's conclusion is very similar to the one we see later, when Jesus has seemingly declared everyone's got to become cannibals by eating his flesh and drinking his blood. Pretty much everyone walked out except the disciples, who had to have been shaken up just as much as Habakkuk was upon hearing the invasion plans. Jesus asks if they will leave, too. "Simon Peter answered him, 'Lord, to whom shall we go? You have the words of eternal life.'"

Surely Peter's response is also that of someone who definitely doesn't understand Jesus' meaning, but who knows Truth when he sees it. He doesn't have to understand the whys and wherefores. Is it easy? No. But sometimes that's all we've got. Trust in God's plan and his love for us.

When the weight of the world is on my shoulders, who do I turn to? When nothing makes sense, can I trust God has my best interests at heart in the long run? Can I be patient with not having control in my life?

Chapter XVII

Balaam

One Bad Prophet and a Smart Ass

And Moses was angry with the officers of the army, the commanders of thousands and the commanders of hundreds, who had come from service in the war. Moses said to them, "Have you let all the women live? Behold, these caused the sons of Israel, by the counsel of Balaam, to act treacherously against the LORD in the matter of Peor, and so the plague came among the congregation of the LORD."

Numbers 31:14–16

What to Read

- Numbers 22:1—24:25; 31:7–16

After all these great Old Testament prophets, let's look at the bad apple among them. (Don't worry, more good stuff coming.)

Jesus Christ himself uses Balaam as a warning to the church in Pergamum in the book of Revelation: "But I have a few things against you: you have some there who hold the teaching of Balaam, who taught Balak to put a stumbling block before the sons of Israel, that they might eat food sacrificed to idols and practice immorality." Centuries after Balaam's prophecies, his name was still a warning. More warnings pop up in Deuteronomy, Joshua,

Micah, Nehemiah, 2 Peter, and Jude. So, yeah, Balaam is a legendarily bad prophet.

Balaam throws into relief for us how surprisingly united Israel's prophets are. Each one's message holds together with the ones that came before. Together, their words weave a clear, cohesive story about God and his continual love. To have such a line of prophets stretching from Abraham to Elijah to John the Baptist is extraordinary. Despite their struggles, they always come back to God in the end.

Balaam, on the other hand, is clearly inspired by God, but prophesies in spite of himself, not because he wants to cooperate. And that makes all the difference.

There's been argument about whether this story is fiction because of the talking donkey. I'm not so sure. For one thing, archaeologists found tablets telling a completely new story about Balaam, son of Beor, just as he is identified in the Bible.* So he did have a powerful reputation. Also, God is hands-on. If he wants a donkey to talk, it's gonna speak up.

Either way, fact or fiction, there's a lot for us to learn from this bad, bad prophet.

Quick Take on Balaam

King Balak's got a huge problem. The Israelites are moving into the promised land, wiping out anyone who gets in their way. Balak's game plan: get powerful pagan prophet and seer, Balaam, to curse the Israelites so his soldiers can mow them down. Balaam's ready (there's a lot of gold and silver mentioned), but God will have none of it. Balaam can go with the king's men, but only if he will do what God tells him. Balaam says, "Of course, we'll do it your way."

But God knows that Balaam doesn't mean it. So God makes his point by sending an angel with a sword to stop Balaam. His

---

* You can actually read it for yourself at https://www.livius.org/sources/content/deir-alla-inscription/

donkey takes one look and shuts the trip down. She (literally) tries to talk sense into Balaam, but he can't see the angel, so he does the only thing he knows — beating and screaming. Finally, the angel with sword appears to Balaam, and that does the trick. Balaam tells Balak that he can't curse what God wants blessed. Balak drags him from place to place to try new sacrifices and curses, hoping a different view might be the solution. Nope. Each blessing is better than the last!

Meanwhile, the Moabite women offer sex and idols to the Israelite men, who just can't say no. This leads to a plague sweeping through the camp. It's not like this is the first time this sort of thing has happened. Sinful cause and punishing effect, guys. Remember?

Deep intel shows the sex and idols are Balaam's master plan. We think he's seen the error of his ways; instead, he finds a loophole by luring God's people to destruction. We don't have time to get too mad, though, because he's killed along with all the other Moabite men. Good riddance!

Living with Balaam

A Tale of Two Asses

Who doesn't love a talking donkey winning an argument? Balaam, that's who.

Balaam's riding with "numerous and distinguished" princes of Moab. They've got a blank check for Balaam if he'll just curse those pesky Israelites. So Balaam makes totally the wrong impression when his donkey suddenly won't do a thing she's supposed to. She turns off the road, crushes his foot into a wall, lies down, and won't move. Now that's embarrassing. I can just hear the jokes about this at every royal event for years. No wonder he's so mad.

The donkey has clearer vision than the great seer Balaam.

The funny part is that the donkey has clearer vision than the great seer Balaam. She sees the angel. He doesn't. She points out that she never acted like this before, but he just yells.

Me, I'd be backing away from a donkey that talked. Balaam's only interested in me, me, me! Honor, wealth, and power are on the line and on his mind. I think we know why God sent an angel with a sword to remind him, "only the word which I bid you, that shall you speak."

This sight finally snaps Balaam into full compliance with God for a little while, under very specific conditions.

In the same way that God sends you down an unexpected road to your heart's desire, he'll also block off another road if it isn't where you should go. That's when it's smart to ask whether God's trying to tell you something. I've had this happen more than once. That dream job that seemed like a sure thing, the true love who left for no reason, the perfect house I've just got to have — all closed roads that I've been grateful for later. God uses unlikely ways to get his message across.

We've got to look and listen and be ready to accept the chance to turn ourselves around. Just the way Balaam didn't.

God's on Your Side — Whether You See It or Not

The Israelites don't have a clue about what's happening with Balaam until later. God's protection is unfailing even when they don't know about it.

They've been praying hard. They're fighting hard. They've won so far. But when did that ever stop anyone from worrying about tomorrow? We know the Israelites are a lot like you and me.

It brings up a curious tightrope we walk. We work and pray toward specific goals. Then, when God doesn't seem to have a hand in things, we wonder why he doesn't care. We don't stop to think that there might be a whole slew of other problems that God's wrangling to get us where we're going.

Look at Balaam's story. What if King Balak had actually listened to Balaam's blessings and decided to welcome the Israelites? Maybe war would have been avoided; the Moabites themselves might have been blessed. What if Balaam had suddenly stopped to wonder more about this God who cares so much about his people? Maybe he could have become a great prophet of God.

God is focused on one goal: blessing the Israelites. But he never turns down side benefits. In fact, he seems to plan for as many as possible. This incident could have changed salvation history in interesting ways. But it didn't. Because not one of the players stopped to think about anything but himself.

In my own case, I'm grateful for all the things I don't need to know about what God's maneuvering to bring about my good. I don't even mind if the wonderful instances I do know about God's love for me in particular are actually side benefits in someone else's grand tale. He's got enough love for everyone.

Escape Clause

God's very clear about what he wants, but Balaam wants a different answer.

Balaam seems to think that all he has to do is reword his argument, maybe sacrifice a few more cows, and God will come around to his way of thinking. I don't know what Balaam's used to, but this is the one true God, not some backwoods Baal. God doesn't go back on his word, and he already made a promise to Abram, long ago: "I will bless those who bless you, and him who curses you I will curse."

To be fair to Balaam, he is used to getting his way. King Balak tells him, "for I know that he whom you bless is blessed, and he whom you curse is cursed." Balaam's been getting that power from somewhere. We tend to dismiss pagan gods as imaginary or wishful thinking, but the biblical understanding is that they are actually demons. Demons are fallen angels who chose evil instead of God's way. What better way to mess people up than using angelic supernatural abilities to bring them to destruction? So if Balaam's used to bargaining with pagan "gods," then he probably assumes the Israelites' God is just more of the same.

Maybe that's why the talking donkey didn't surprise him.

Balaam demonstrates a sneering contempt for God when he finds a loophole to "curse" the Israelites. "Hey, you didn't tell me not to send a little Moabite entertainment for the troops." God gives a definitive lesson here on who is the real source of blessings and curses.

Doesn't this sound familiar? I try to convince God that my happiness matters more than pleasing him, that what I want is what I should get. I keep trying to change his mind. What I'm not doing, just like Balaam, is listening. I know I don't want to hear what God would tell me. Because what I want isn't really that bad, is it?

I can lie to myself, but I'm not fooling God. And I know it. I don't want to be like Balaam. I want a right relationship with God. I've got the examples of God's faithful prophets to show me the better way. Listening to God, cooperating with God, loving God, will help me avoid winding up like Balaam.

Chapter XVIII

Anna and Simeon

God's Tag Team

Now there was a man in Jerusalem, whose name was Simeon, and this man was righteous and devout, looking for the consolation of Israel, and the Holy Spirit was upon him. She [Anna] did not depart from the temple, worshiping with fasting and prayer night and day.

Luke 2:25, 37

What to Read

- Luke 2:22–38

It blows my mind thinking that this story was told to Luke by Mary herself. Think about it. By the time Luke was writing his gospel, only Mary was left alive. When Luke says, "But Mary kept all these things, pondering them in her heart," you can take that to the bank.

You know how when the old-timers come up and want to talk your ear off about the good old days, you start looking for the exit? Back in biblical times, it was different. The Torah's word for elderly also means "wise." Everyone knew the old-timers had seen it all, and had the experience to break down the real meaning of things. When they began talking, everyone listened.

So when Anna and Simeon begin proclaiming about Jesus,

Mary and Joseph know this is something out of the ordinary. Simeon's righteous, and Anna's a prophetess. They're holy veterans who've seen plenty of false messiahs, fake prophets, and corrupt officials betray the faithful time after time. Still, they trust in God. Chances are they're well known enough that when the Holy Spirit tugs at their hearts over this anonymous mother and baby, everyone moves in for a look-see.

Quick Take on Anna and Simeon

Mary and Joseph take Baby Jesus to the temple in Jerusalem for the ritual purification and sacrifice after a firstborn son.

Before they even get started, old Simeon bursts on the scene and takes Baby Jesus into his arms. He lifts his voice in praise, echoing Isaiah's long-ago prophecy: "I will give you as a light to the nations, that my salvation may reach to the end of the earth." This is God's salvation, the Messiah. This is what the Holy Spirit's been keeping Simeon alive to experience. Or rather, not "what" but "who." Surely Simeon is the first to realize that God's salvation ("Jesus" means "God saves") is this baby, someone into whose eyes he is looking from just a few inches away.

Enter Anna. She's an aged prophetess living a super-holy life by fasting and praying around the clock at the temple. She takes one look and finishes connecting the dots by pointing to the future, when this baby will redeem Jerusalem.

This is Mary and Joseph's third set of witnesses, after the shepherds and the wise men, to Jesus' remarkable destiny. Needless to say, they're amazed at yet another revelation from God about their son.

But the people of Israel haven't heard the news until now. The Holy Spirit uses this aged dynamic duo to announce to the general population that the long wait is over. God is acting, and his salvation is all wrapped up in this little tyke.

Living with Anna and Simeon

That's One Sassy Granny

OK, maybe she's not sassy. Or actually a granny. But Anna's got spunk, and she's not a quitter. She's eighty-four and prays and fasts all day and night. For decades.

These days we might say that someone who spends decades just praying and fasting is missing out on real life. But Anna doesn't see it as a waste of time. She's important. She matters. For one thing, she's the only woman in the New Testament, and one of the few characters there at all, with a tribal listing. In fact, she's one of only a handful of women in the entire Bible recognized as "prophetess."*

Anna's prophetic vocation to prayer is viewed as important in and of itself.

Anna isn't arranging flowers or teaching Sabbath school, which is how I think of eighty-four-year-old ladies spending their time at church. Her prophetic vocation to prayer is viewed as important in and of itself. She doesn't have to "produce" anything in order to be of value to God or to others.

Have I fallen into the American habit of thinking that action matters most of all? Even when I can't see direct results, do I take prayer seriously? Do I believe God will use my prayers? Is there value in prayer for its own sake? This is a problem in a results-oriented society, and it makes me realize that I often don't trust God to handle my vocation the way Anna does.

When You Ask for a Messiah and God Gives You … a Baby?

Luke tells us that "his father and his mother marveled at what was said about him." After angels and shepherds, a star and foreign wise men, you'd think Mary and Joseph would be used to miraculous announcements dropping onto them right and left.

---

* The other prophetesses are Miriam (Ex 15:20), Deborah (Jgs 4:4); Huldah (2 Chr 34:22), the mother of Isaiah's son (Is 8:3), and Philip's four daughters (Acts 21:9).

Of course, they can't possibly know the full implications of this miraculous birth. Complete acceptance of God's will is one thing. Complete understanding often comes later. That is definitely the case before Jesus' actual ministry, death on the cross, and resurrection.

A lot of the time we understand something only when we look back. We realize that we didn't have a clue at the time about the big picture. I've struggled with those things before. When I first became Catholic, I struggled with Church teachings on many social issues, such as gay marriage, abortion, and the death penalty. It took a lot of reading and reflection before I was able to see the logic behind the teachings, though it was bitterly hard in some cases to understand why the Church taught what she did. Better understanding gradually came as I pondered.

Anna and Simeon themselves can't understand all that this tiny Messiah will bring, but they trust God enough to make their announcements to the amazed parents. What a beautiful example we're given: Mary was so open with Luke that all his readers are told she and Joseph didn't understand everything all the time. They, like us, also had to puzzle out what was going on, trust God, and do their best every day.

The D-Word

> "Lord, now let your servant depart in peace,
> according to your word;
> for my eyes have seen your salvation
> which you have prepared in the presence of all
> peoples,
> a light for revelation to the Gentiles,
> and for glory to your people Israel." (Lk 2:29–32)

Simeon has been told he won't die until he sees the Messiah. He seems pretty excited now. Not only has God kept his promise to Israel, but also because the prophesy comes with, "let your servant depart in peace." Is he sick or feeble or just ready for the next step? We don't know.

Anna doesn't mention death, but at eighty-four she's got to know it can't be far away. After all, her husband died when they'd only been married seven years, and her whole life afterward has been affected by that reality.

Let's face it: None of us is getting out of here alive. Death is a reality we can't avoid, though our society does its level best. In Anna and Simeon's day, death and suffering were something you saw all the time. These days, we are barely prepared to deal with the loss of a loved one, much less think about our own ends. Christian communities used to spend a good amount of time talking about the "last things" to help Christians keep their eyes on the prize, but even that is done much less these days.

In my own case, it took a cancer biopsy to make me face reality. I sat in the waiting room, face-to-face with the fact that I will definitely die someday. That idea had never been so real to me, thinking, "Jesus, I am counting on you to be there to help me." Suddenly, in my mind's eye came a vision of a closed white door with a green light shining from a crack at the bottom. It was vividly springlike and indescribably exciting. I could tell there was something completely new on the other side. Now, when the reality of my death comes to mind, I fall back on that memory.

I understand now what Peter Pan meant when he said, "To die will be an awfully big adventure." Maybe that's how Simeon feels, too — ready for the big adventure.

Thinking about death reminds us all to make sure we live our lives well. Am I living up to my potential? Do I have regrets that I can atone for now? Do I try to love Jesus more every day?

What do you want to be like at the end of your life? Will you be ready for the big adventure when it comes?

Chapter XIX

John the Baptist

He's Got One Job. Just Try to Stop Him.

And when Elizabeth heard the greeting of Mary, the child leaped in her womb; and Elizabeth was filled with the Holy Spirit and she exclaimed with a loud cry, "Blessed are you among women, and blessed is the fruit of your womb! And why is this granted me, that the mother of my Lord *should come to me? For behold, when the voice of your greeting came to my ears, the child in my womb leaped for joy."*

Luke 1:41–44

What to Read

All four Gospels talk about John the Baptist, but in slightly different ways.

- Matthew 3; 11:2–14; 14:1–12
- Mark 1:1–11; 6:14–29
- Luke 1; 3:1–22; 7:18–23
- John 1:6–37; 3:22–36

Announcing the Messiah is the job John was born to do. He begins before he's even born, signaling his mother from the womb when he leaps for joy because unborn Jesus is nearby.

It's been four hundred years since the last prophet. If you're tracking Daniel's prophesy of 490 years after rebuilding the temple — and a lot of people are — then it's time for the Messiah to show up. Plenty of would-be messiahs are out there, but none of them is the real deal. John's job is to prepare the people so everyone will recognize Jesus.

John stands as the connection between the Old and New Testaments. He's the last of the Old Covenant prophets, but when this guy says the Messiah's coming, he means here and now. Every one of the Gospels features him kicking off Jesus' ministry, and then stepping out of the spotlight as Jesus revs up.

John's life is interwoven with Jesus'. It's go time, and God's making sure the loose ends are tied up. If we don't pick up on this, then we're just not paying attention. Both of their stories begin with an angelic announcement, an unlikely conception, and a miraculous birth. Also, they're cousins, born six months apart. And that's just the beginning.

Quick Take on John the Baptist

Zechariah the priest is at the altar of the temple in Jerusalem when the angel Gabriel appears with great news that a son will be born to him, even though he and his wife are way too old. Also, they should name the baby John.

Fast forward: John, now grown, comes in from the desert. I can see the scene in slow motion: epic music, big strides with staff in hand, people turning and dropping things to follow him. The camera pans over his tanned face, his clothes of camel's hair, his food (locusts and wild honey — ugh). It works. The people know classic Old Testament prophet style when they see it. And in case they don't, John uses Scripture combining Isaiah, Malachi, and Exodus to remind them. This is the messenger, the voice in the wilderness, who will announce the Messiah.

Just a sec — let me catch my breath.

John proclaims a baptism of repentance for the forgiveness of sins. The Jewish people love him. They're lining up for dunking in the Jordan River. The religious officials … not so much. This baptism is the sort that only Gentiles need, not the Jews, right? They want to know what's the point, but John's not interested in making them happy. He just says another will come after him who will not baptize with water, but with the Holy Spirit.

John also proclaims forgiveness, fair dealings with everyone, and sharing with the poor. He's got a real Jesus-vibe, but we haven't met Jesus yet. We are dying to meet him, though, so John's stuff is working. And then — surprise! — Jesus shows up in line for baptism. John is shocked. He says that he should ask Jesus to baptize him instead, but Jesus insists. The Holy Spirit descends on Jesus like a dove, and a voice from heaven says "Thou art my beloved Son; with thee I am well pleased."

Jesus is in action now, and some of John's disciples follow him instead. John's cool. He knows who's the Messiah and who isn't. He keeps on baptizing and preaching until a certain King Herod's wife gets upset because she doesn't want the truth about her second marriage shouted in the streets. John's arrested and, surprisingly, Herod takes to visiting him for philosophical chats.

Things come to a head when Herod's stepdaughter Salome dances as dinner entertainment, and Herod promises her whatever she wants. Her mother's prepped her. Salome asks for John the Baptist's head on a platter, and Herod's too chicken to back down in front of company. So John is killed for upsetting the local political establishment. Catch that Jesus-vibe again? Foreshadowing, thy name is John. Truly, his entire life was given in service of God and the Messiah.

Living with John the Baptist

Putting in the Time

John shows us *righteous* in practical terms. He's baptizing and truth-telling. If people don't agree, he shrugs it off. Cut off his head for telling the truth? He's not crazy about the plan, but you gotta do what you gotta do. And right up to that moment, he's going to keep on with his mission.

John knows who he is, which means he's humble. He knows whom he can trust, because he's close to God. You can't spend something like fifteen years in the desert without coming out humble and trusting.

I'd love to be more like John, though I draw the line at eating bugs, even with honey. I do long to be that trusting and close to God. That means the hard stuff: prayer.

How do you pray? All through my day I rattle off little bits of prayer: "Help me be more patient ... Show me how to talk to this angry person ... Thank you for that parking space!" (Hey, God cares about my parking ... sometimes.) But that's not enough, and I feel it when I don't put in the personal time to connect more.

Sometimes the hard part is just beginning. Here's the list I use to regroup when I need to regain that regular prayer habit:

- Schedule a regular time. Try for fifteen or twenty minutes.
- Pray even if I don't want to.
- Prayer isn't about "results," so relax.
- There's not just one kind of prayer. Use whatever helps open up conversation and inspiration: Scripture reading, nature, music, art, imagining scenes from the Gospels.
- Listen. Prayer is a conversation, so be sure to give God his turn.

I come back to these guidelines again and again. Which brings up the last one: never quit trying.

Always the Best Man, Never the Groom

It would be easy for John to get his head turned. He's gone viral. People are coming from a long way away for baptism. Rumor is that he's the Messiah, or at least Elijah returned.

When Jesus shows up and some of John's disciples jump

ship, a lesser man might be jealous or angry. But nothing distracts this guy. John just says, "He must increase, but I must decrease."

How does he stay so chill?

We don't get a lot of clues, because John doesn't talk about himself much. But at one point, John says he's overjoyed because he's the best man at the wedding. A first-century best man is a busy guy. He's the liaison between the groom and bride, arranges the ceremony, handles invitations, and presides at the wedding feast. His top job is to guard the bridal bedroom door — in the dark. When he hears the groom's voice, he lets him in.

Anyone who's helped at a wedding knows about joyful, selfless service to make someone's special day perfect. John gets Israel and Jesus together. Who wouldn't be happy about that?

John gets Israel and Jesus together. Who wouldn't be happy about that?

Of course, it's easy to rejoice when there's a big special event to prepare for. What about every day? How does "I must decrease" work the rest of the time? Like John, I have to keep my eye on the big picture, my goal of getting to heaven and helping my family get there. Of being a help and not a hindrance to friends and those around me — they need to get to heaven, too. Of being a saint. In the end, that's the big picture I have to remember when I'm tempted to think it's all about me instead of all about Christ.

Still The One

Nothing shakes John. Almost nothing.

"Now when John heard in prison about the deeds of the Christ, he sent word by his disciples and said to him, 'Are you he who is to come, or shall we look for another?' And Jesus answered them, 'Go and tell John what you hear and see: the blind receive their sight and the lame walk, lepers are cleansed and the deaf hear, and the dead are raised up, and the poor have good news preached to them. And blessed is he who takes no offense at me.'"

You can't blame John for double-checking that Jesus is "the One." We don't know what John himself was expecting. We do know that Jesus isn't doing what a lot of people think of as Messiah-ish stuff. He's eating with tax collectors. He's accused of being a glutton and a drunk. He's talking to women in public. Oy vey!

I love Jesus' answer. He says to tell John the results of his actions. We're pointed right back at Isaiah's predictions. Jesus and John both know them by heart. That has to be the most reassuring message John could have gotten; he might not understand the other stuff, but these miracles connect back to the heart of the prophetic message.

God understands when we have questions or doubts. The key is to honestly go to him with those struggles. His plan ranges way beyond our limited vision, and it's easy to get confused. We've all been there. Heck, that's why the Catholic Church has two thousand years of thinking about the same kinds of doubts and questions we have now. Saint Augustine, for example, scolded people for not bothering to know current science, because that made them sound stupid to non-Christians. And in the *Summa Theologica,* Saint Thomas Aquinas considers whether wet dreams are sinful (short answer: no, but it could be because of a previous sin). Truly, there is nothing under the sun that hasn't been asked.

So we've got questions. God's got answers. Speak up. He won't mind.

Chapter XX

Jesus

Door to New Life

I led you out of Egypt, from slavery to freedom,
but you led your Savior to the cross.
I opened the sea before you,
but you opened my side with a spear.
I led you on your way in a pillar of cloud,
but you led me to Pilate's court.

The Reproaches

As I was sitting in church on Good Friday during the veneration of the cross, the Reproaches rang in my ears, beautifully and mournfully sung by our choir in notes evoking the ancient Middle East. Suddenly my mind's eye saw, stretching back behind the cross, the long line of prophets who preceded this moment when God stepped into history.

It brought tears to my eyes. It does again as I write these words.

Millennia of striving, showing, coaxing, to open our hearts to the reality of God's love for us. It ends in the cross, Jesus' act of ultimate love. The prophets' witness gives reality and full meaning to Jesus' mourning: "Jerusalem, Jerusalem, you who kill the prophets and stone those sent to you, how many times I yearned to gather your children together, as a hen gathers her young under her wings, but you were unwilling!"

We feel it. We know it. We've just seen the prophets' witness to God's continual love.

I feel as if I know the prophets' struggle in a whole new way. Surrounded by uncaring pagans and even more uncaring Israelites, they didn't stand a chance. No matter how flamboyant or tearful or miraculous they were, they were lone voices in the wilderness. But God works his biggest miracles when the stakes are highest, right? He uses weak, faithful people who don't stand a chance, but who step forward in faith.

We, too, are surrounded by an uncaring pagan culture. They've got their idols all right, but they can't see how misguided they are. The prophets would understand. Human nature hasn't changed since their time. We've got advanced methods, but they'd recognize our motives, our restless search for happiness and understanding and love.

The prophets wouldn't have come across sex-change operations, but they'd understand being so unhappy that you'd grasp at anything to fix your life. They wouldn't fathom transhumanism, which wants to push the human race to a new evolutionary level with nanobots, uploading consciousness to computers, personality pills, or other advanced technology. But they'd understand the desire for immortality and god-like knowledge.

Would the prophets recognize that Jesus is the Messiah? I don't know. They got tiny glimpses, each with a different vantage point. Jesus isn't what anyone expected. His life, death, and resurrection flip human expectations upside down. We see that in the Gospels. But they'd definitely understand being surprised by God. He's so big, and we're so limited — we'll always be surprised by him. They know that for sure.

Jesus' resurrection is out-of-the-box thinking. Not only because he comes back from the dead, but also because he is such a changed type of human. The disciples don't recognize him, as he walks through locked doors, vanishes in the blink of an eye, and is unlimited by time or space. Pope Benedict XVI points out in *Jesus of Nazareth: Holy Week** that this is the next phase of humanity, the "evolutionary leap" that God intended all along, but which human stubbornness, pride, and sin threw off track:

> Jesus' Resurrection was about breaking out into an entirely new form of life, into a life that is no longer subject to the law of dying and becoming, but lies beyond it — a life that opens up a new dimension of human existence. Therefore the Resurrection of Jesus is not an isolated event that we could set aside as something limited to the past, but it constitutes an "evolutionary leap" ... that affects everyone and that opens up a future, a new kind of future, for mankind. Indeed, matter itself is remolded into a new type of reality. ... opening up a dimension that affects us all, creating for all of us a new space of life, a new space of being in union with God.

These thoughts about the Resurrection emphasize the trajectory of salvation history — God's action in human history for our redemption. The prophets come first to get our attention, so that we'll recognize the Messiah. Jesus the Messiah loves you and me so much that he becomes man and suffers on the cross in order to redeem us for that transformation into new life. The next big event, the showstopper, will be the Second Coming, when Christ returns to earth at the end of human history.

But until the Second Coming, there is still a job to do. Jesus told his disciples to go and spread the Good News. So, as his disciples, it's our turn to jump in. This is where we go on our side of the cross, after the Resurrection, forward with Jesus' message to the world. He made you for this moment, placed you here as part of his plan — to act, to speak truth, to step forward with courage and love. It's our turn to open the door for Christ.

---

* Pope Benedict XVI, *Jesus of Nazareth: From the Entrance into Jerusalem to the Resurrection* (San Francisco: Ignatius Press, 2011).

What to Read

Once you're acquainted with the prophets, it's fascinating to see how they pop up in the New Testament.

- Luke 24:13–35 — My favorite Resurrection story, because it begins with Jesus teaching a Bible study on the road to Emmaus, "beginning with Moses and all the prophets, he interpreted to them in all the scriptures the things concerning himself," which helps inspire the disciples to recognize him.
- Hebrews 11 — This is salvation history in a nutshell, beginning with Abel, including the prophets, and ending with Christ.
- Matthew 22:37–40 — Jesus says all the law and the prophets hang on two things. When you're reading the prophets, do you see why he says that?
- Romans 3:21 — Goes hand in hand with Matthew 22:37.

Of course, Jesus knew the prophets like the back of his hand, especially as they pertained to him. He often quotes one or even mashes a couple together and updates the meaning by applying it to a new situation. I mentioned a few already in this book, but here are a few others. These are fun to think about and also show how important the prophets are to Jesus' teachings. Check out some of his mentions with the original prophetic text.

- Matthew 10:35–36, Luke 12:52–53 = Micah 7:6
- Matthew 11:10, Luke 7:27 = Malachi 3:1
- Matthew 13:14–15, Mark 4:11–13, Lk 8:10 = Isaiah 6:9–10
- Matthew 21:13, Mark 11:17, Luke 19:46 = Isaiah 56:7 plus Jeremiah 7:11
- Matthew 21:42, Mark 12:10, Luke 20:17 = Psalm

118:22–23
- John 13:18 = Psalm 41:9
- Matthew 9:13 = Hosea 6:6

Want more? Many Catholic Bibles and commentaries list the cross-references between Old Testament and New Testament. When you start using those footnotes, that's when the work really comes alive in the way it is pointing forward and backward at Jesus' presence in the whole Bible.

Basic Resources

A Few of My Favorite Books

Bible Overview

Inside the Bible: An Introduction to Each Book of the Bible, by Father Kenneth Baker, S.J.
One of my go-to books for good biblical overview. It covers the basics of each scriptural text: author, date, theme, outline, and summary. The brief theological explanation can also be helpful.

You Can Understand the Bible: A Practical Guide to Each Book in the Bible, by Peter Kreeft
Kreeft fleshes out his biblical overview with insights into how to apply each book to modern life and how to make the book come alive for the imagination. He's also funny.

Scriptural Commentary

Ignatius Catholic Study Bible, by Scott Hahn and Curtis Mitch
Copious footnotes in this edition bring out elements of Scripture that you may have missed before. Solid scholarship connects the comments with Catholic theology in a very accessible way. It's currently a work in progress. The New Testament is finished and available in one volume; the Old Testament books are being published individually as the authors finish them.

The Navarre Bible, Scepter Publishers
The Navarre commentaries are consistently excellent and in-

clude thoughts from Church Fathers, popes, saints, and the *Catechism*. This is where you're going to get a look at the consistency of Catholic scriptural commentary over the last two thousand years.

The Hebrew Bible, translated by Robert Alter
Alter is an expert in ancient Hebrew. His translation and commentary vividly bring Scripture alive from the Jewish perspective. The commentary is cultural and literary rather than religious. You'll find a few books missing — this is the Hebrew Bible, and some of the Old Testament was written in Greek. This isn't a Catholic work, so feel free to disagree with some of his interpretations, but he gets you thinking. You can find Alter's translations in individual books or as a three-volume (expensive) set.

Catholic Commentary on Sacred Scripture, Baker Academic
This series takes you through each New Testament book, little by little. It combines a lot of the information that can be found in a variety of other commentaries (both Catholic and Protestant), but then pulls it all together with additional observations that make it accessible.

Cultural Backgrounds Study Bible: Bringing to Life the Ancient World of Scripture, Zondervan
This book explains the basics of the Bible's cultural backgrounds through the lens of ancient history, archaeology, and literature. It's a Protestant study, which means it doesn't include some of the books Catholics have as part of the scriptural canon.

People of the New Testament

The Apostles, by Pope Benedict XVI
Once a teacher, always a teacher. Pope Benedict preached a long series of teaching homilies, beginning with the apostles. He looks at the life of each apostle, using him as a springboard for

examining our own lives and relationship to Christ. These are not about the prophets whom we were discussing in the book, but they do help see how to look at other biblical characters in the same way. Other books in the series compile the pope's homilies on particular themes, including *The Fathers* (two volumes), *Doctors of the Church, Holy Women, Great Teachers, Saint Paul,* and *Prayer* (which also discusses some of the prophets you've met in this book).

Prayer

The Art of Praying: The Principles and Methods of Christian Prayer, by Romano Guardini

Praying is hard. But when we approach the Scriptures, we're meant to be praying, listening to God's word and responding to him. This little book has loads of practical, common-sense tips for prayer, as well as deep insights about God that have influenced me greatly. I keep it on my Kindle for daily reading before I pick up my Bible during my prayer time.

Scripture Quotations

Classic Lines

I get distracted when every time there's a Scripture quote, there's that attribution in parentheses right behind it. But sometimes I'd like to know where those great lines are from. Here's the scoop for all the stuff that's uncredited in the chapters. All Scripture is from the Revised Standard Version, Second Catholic Edition, unless otherwise noted.

Moses

God called to him out of the bush, "Moses, Moses!" And he said, "Here am I." (Ex 3:4)

"Let my people go." (Ex 5:1)

Now the man Moses was very humble, more than anyone else on earth. (Nm 12:3, NABRE)

"Would it not be better for us to go back to Egypt?" (Nm 14:3)

Miriam

Let the greatest among you be as the youngest, and the leader as the servant. (Lk 22:26, NABRE)

Has the LORD indeed spoken only through Moses? Has he not spoken through us also? (Nm 12:2)

Deborah

Out of the window she peered,
the mother of Sisera gazed through the lattice:
"Why is his chariot so long in coming?
Why do the hoofbeats of his chariots tarry?" (Jgs 5:28)

So on that day God subdued Jabin the king of Canaan before the sons of Israel. (Jgs 4:23)

I will draw out Sisera, the general of Jabin's army, to meet you by the river Kishon with his chariots and his troops; and I will give him into your hand. (Jgs 4:7)

Out of weakness they were made powerful, became strong in battle, and turned back foreign invaders. (Heb 11:34, NABRE)

Samuel

Like all the nations (1 Sam 8:5, NABRE)

Many are called, but few are chosen. (Mt 22:14)

The LORD God took the man and put him in the garden of Eden to till it and keep it. (Gn 2:15)

David

"Being therefore a prophet, and knowing that God had sworn with an oath to him that he would set one of his descendants upon his throne, he foresaw and spoke of the resurrection of the Christ, that he was not abandoned to Hades, nor did his flesh see corruption." (Acts 2:30–31)

He who sang as none other sang in Israel. Through me the spirit of the LORD has spoken; his words are on my tongue. (2 Kgs 23:2, The Knox Bible)

My God, my God, why have you abandoned me? (Ps 22:2, NABRE)

I am poured out like water,
    and all my bones are out of joint;
my heart is like wax,
    it is melted within my breast. (Ps 22:14)

You have turned my mourning into dancing;
    you have loosed my sackcloth
        and clothed me with gladness,
    that my soul may praise you and not be silent.
        O LORD my God, I will give thanks to you for ever. (Ps 30:11–12)

Nathan

You are the man. (2 Sm 12:7)

Elijah

But [insert king's name here] did what was evil in the LORD's sight, more than any of his predecessors. (1 Kgs 16:30, NABRE)

Then [Elijah] was afraid, and he arose and went for his life. (1 Kgs 19:3)

"I, even I only, am left; and they seek my life." (1 Kgs 19:10)

What are you doing here, Elijah? (1 Kgs 19:9)

"stand upon the mount before the LORD." (1 Kgs 19:11)

As the LORD your God, lives, I have nothing baked. (1 Kgs 17:12)

"Now I know that you are a man of God, and that the word of the LORD in your mouth is truth." (1 Kgs 17:24)

Elisha

He went up from there to Bethel; and while he was going up on the way, some small boys came out of the city and jeered at him, saying, "Go up, you baldhead! Go up, you baldhead!" And he turned around, and when he saw them, he cursed them in the name of the LORD. And two she-bears came out of the woods and tore forty-two of the boys. (2 Kgs 2:23–25)

Isaiah

Today this Scripture has been fulfilled in your hearing. (Lk 4:21)
"Whom shall I send and who will go for us? … Here I am! Send me." (Is 6:8)

Come now, let us reason together,
says the LORD:
though your sins are like scarlet,
they shall be as white as snow;
though they are red like crimson,
they shall become like wool. (Is 1:18)

"Woe is me! For I am lost; for I am a man of unclean lips." (Is 6:5)

"Depart from me, for I am a sinful man, O Lord." (Lk 5:8)

Then the eyes of the blind shall be opened,
and the ears of the deaf unstopped;
then shall the lame man leap like a hart,
and the tongue of the mute sing for joy. (Is 35:5–6)

Jeremiah

You seduced me, Lord, and I let myself be seduced. (Jer 20:7, NABRE)

Cursed be the day
on which I was born! (Jer 20:14)

You will seek me and find me; when you seek me with all your heart. (Jer 29:13)

Now the word of the LORD came to me saying,
"Before I formed you in the womb I knew you,
and before you were born I consecrated you;
I appointed you a prophet to the nations." (Jer 1:4–5)

Ezekiel

Have I any pleasure in the death of the wicked, says the Lord God, and not rather that he should turn from his way and live? ... For I have no pleasure in the death of any one, says the Lord God; so turn, and live. (Ez 18:23, 32)

A new heart I will give you, and a new spirit I will put within you; and I will take out of your flesh the heart of stone and give you a heart of flesh. (Ez 36:26)

Daniel

Put on the whole armor of God, that you may be able to stand against the wiles of the devil. (Eph 6:11)

thorn in the flesh, messenger of Satan (2 Cor 12:7)

Taking his stand in the midst of them, [Daniel] said, "Are you such fools, you sons of Israel? Have you condemned a daughter of Israel without examination and without learning the facts? Return to the place of judgment. For these men have borne false witness against her." ... And Daniel said to them, "Separate them far from each other, and I will examine them." (Dn 13:48–49, 51)

Hosea

The LORD said to Hosea: "Go, get for yourself a woman of prostitution and children of prostitution, for the land prostitutes itself, turning away from the LORD." (Hos 1:2, NABRE)

If any man would come after me, let him deny himself and take up his cross and follow me. (Mt 16:24)

Amos

Remember the sabbath day, to keep it holy. Six days you shall labor, and do all your work; but the seventh day is a sabbath to the Lord your God; in it you shall not do any work. (Ex 20:8–10)

Jonah

"The LORD, the LORD, a God merciful and gracious, slow to anger, and abounding in mercy and faithfulness, keeping merciful love for thousands, forgiving iniquity and transgression and sin, but who will by no means clear the guilty." (Ex 34:6–7)

"Is not this what I said when I was yet in my country? That is why I made haste to flee to Tarshish; for I knew that you are a gracious God and merciful, slow to anger, and abounding in mercy, and that you repent of evil." (Jon 4:2)

And the LORD said … "And should not I pity Nineveh, that great city, in which there are more than a hundred and twenty thousand persons who do not know their right hand from their left, and also much cattle?" (Jon 4:10–11)

"Father, forgive them, for they know not what they do." (Lk 23:34)

Habakkuk

The just one who is righteous because of his faith shall live. (Hb 2:4, NABRE)

I will take my stand to watch,
and station myself on the tower,
and look forth to see what he will say to me,
and what I will answer concerning my complaint. (Hb 2:1)

For still the vision awaits its time;
    it hastens to the end — it will not lie.
If it seem slow, wait for it;
    it will surely come, it will not delay. (Hb 2:3)

I hear, and my body trembles, my lips quiver at the sound; rottenness enters into my bones, my steps totter beneath me. (Hb 3:16)

Simon Peter answered him, "Lord, to whom shall we go? You have the words of eternal life." (Jn 6:68)

Balaam

But I have a few things against you: you have some there who hold the teaching of Balaam, who taught Balak to put a stumbling block before the sons of Israel, that they might eat food sacrificed to idols and practice immorality. (Rv 2:14)

"Only the word which I bid you, that shall you speak." (Nm 22:35)

"I will bless those who bless you, and him who curses you I will curse." (Gn 12:3)

"For I know that he whom you bless is blessed, and he whom you curse is cursed." (Nm 22:6)

Anna and Simeon

But Mary kept all these things, pondering them in her heart. (Lk 2:19)

"I will give you as a light to the nations,
that my salvation may reach to the end of the earth." (Is 49:6)

His father and his mother marveled at what was said about him. (Lk 2:33)

"Lord, now lettest thou thy servant depart in peace,
according to thy word;
for my eyes have seen your salvation
which you have prepared in the presence of all peoples,
a light for revelation to the Gentiles,
and for glory to thy people Israel." (Lk 2:29–32)

John the Baptist

"You are my beloved Son; with you I am well pleased." (Mk 1:11)

"He must increase, but I must decrease." (Jn 3:30)

"Are you he who is to come, or shall we look for another?" And Jesus answered them, "Go and tell John what you hear and see: the blind receive their sight and the lame walk, lepers are cleansed and the deaf hear, and the dead are raised up, and the poor have good news preached to them. And blessed is he who takes no offense at me." (Mt 11:2–6)

Jesus

"Jerusalem, Jerusalem, you who kill the prophets and stone those sent to you, how many times I yearned to gather your children together, as a hen gathers her young under her wings, but you were unwilling!" (Mt 23:37, NABRE)

Special Thanks

I'd like to thank the people who read the first draft, arguing and questioning as they went: Rose Davis, Scott Danielson, Will Duquette, Patsy Edinburgh.

Sincere thanks to Mary Beth Baker for seeing the germ of this book hidden within my initial book submission.

Thanks to Rebecca Willen, the politest questioner I've met. And one who kept me on my toes defending my assertions.

And, of course, all my love and thanks to Tom — always.

About the Author

Julie Davis and her husband live in Dallas, Texas, and have worked together at their graphic design firm for thirty-one years. They also have a small business doing movie discussion groups with senior communities, called Talking Movies. They have two grown daughters.

Julie converted to Catholicism in 2000 and began blogging at *Happy Catholic* in 2004. That precipitated her entry into both the Catholic internet world and social media, where she has been very involved.

Her book *Happy Catholic* was published in April 2011, and *Lord, Open My Heart* was published in December 2011. She self-published *Seeking Jesus in Everyday Life* in 2017.